A MANUAL ON
PROJECT MANAGEMENT

G.L. TIKU

ATLANTIC
PUBLISHERS & DISTRIBUTORS

Published by
ATLANTIC PUBLISHERS AND DISTRIBUTORS
B-2, Vishal Enclave, Opp. Rajouri Garden, New Delhi-27
Phones : 5413460, 5429987, 5466842

Sales Office
4215/1, Ansari Road, Darya Ganj, New Delhi-110 002
Phones : 3273880, 3285873, 3280451
Fax : 91-11-3285873
e-mail : info@atlanticbooks.com
web : www.atlanticbooks.com

ISBN 81-269-0179-9

Typeset at
APD Computer Graphics, Delhi
Printed in India at
Nice Printing Press, Delhi

PREFACE

We have been witnessing phenomenal growth in the industrial activities in the country for the past decade or so. This has led to the ushering in rapid economic progress which has resulted in an improved quality of life.

With the advent of open economy, more and more multinational companies are encouraged to set up their manufacturing bases in the country to meet the ever-growing domestic demands. This has a salutary effect upon the local business houses as well, by helping to build up a competitive edge, by bringing in the latest developments in technology and to meet the growing market competition.

As very little documented guidance on Project Management Science is available at present, I, having been associated with the formulation and execution of large industrial projects in the recent past, seek to fill in the void to some extent by writing this book entitled, *A Manual of Project Management*.

When the task or job on-hand reaches a certain proportion of size and complexity, there is a need for lateral or "across the lines" co-ordination essential for its success. This additional management is usually termed as 'Project Management'. Its function primarily is to drive the project forward as a project; line management by definition must concern itself with its line function tasks.

Project Management comprises two things : A management arrangement and a system of management techniques. The book deals within all aspects, beginning from the stage of preparations of the project proposal to its successful implementation.

This book could never have seen the light of the day, but for the faith reposed in me by my previous employer — The Premier Automobiles Ltd., Mumbai, by appointing me as a Chief Project Manager for its prestigious project, New Car Assembly Project. I would like to acknowledge my gratefulness to the management of Premier Automobiles for this.

I would like to put on record my deep sense of gratitude to my wife, Krishna, who stood patiently by me during the completion of this onerous task. I would also like to thank my daughters, Sagorika and Anupama, for their invaluable assistance and encouragement in bringing forth the book in its present form.

G.L. TIKU

CONTENTS

1
Introduction

Of late, Project Management Science has increasingly played a major role in evaluating capital expenditure proposals that have been developed by financial economists. Often, the *ad hoc* procedures and rules of thumb, erstwhile employed by businessmen, are not compatible with the scarce resources.

During past few decades, rapid industrialization and construction activities with high prone risk element, has given duc impetus to the role, which project management science has come to play, to improve project appraisal and capital budgeting in practice.

A project can be defined as a scientifically evolved work plan devised to achieve a specific objective within a specified period of time. Taken in this perspective, while projects can differ in size, nature, objectives and complexity, they must all partake of three basic attributes of being a course of action; of having specific objectives; and of involving a definite time perspective. The work plan must lay down in clear and unambiguous terms the manner in which the pre-defined project objectives are to be achieved, the resources which will be consumed in the process of achieving, the objectives and also the time that will be required for achieving the objectives.

From the point of view of resource allocation, a project can be considered as a proposal involving capital investment for the purpose of developing facilities to provide goods or services. The goods or services which the project seeks to provide differ widely. A project may involve the establishment of a new facilities for manufacture of goods, it may involve the provision of additional facilities to a particular age group in the community, or it may aim at developing infrastructure facilities for marketing commodities. Whatever the nature of a project, a project will involve allocation and consumption of resources on one hand and generation of resources, goods or services on the other hand.

Projects have been classified in various ways by different authorities. Little and Mirrlees divide projects into two broad categories *viz.*, quantifiable projects and non-quantifiable projects. Quantifiables are those in which a plausible quantitative assessment of benefits can be made. Non-quantifiables are those where such assessment is not feasible. Projects concerned with industrial development, power generation, mineral development fall in the first category while projects involving health, education and defence, fall in the second category.

The Planning Commission in India has accepted the Sectorial bias as the criteria for classification of projects. A project may, under this classification, fall into any one of the following sectors: Agriculture and allied sectors; irrigation and power; industry and mining; transport and communication; social services; and miscellaneous sectors.

This system of classification has been found useful in resource allocation at the macro level. Projects are sometimes classified on the basis of their techno-economic characteristics. These main groups of classification can be identified as : Factor Intensity Oriented; Causation Oriented ; and Magnitude Oriented.

Under Factor Intensity, projects are classified as capital intensive or labor intensive depending upon large-scale investment in plant and machinery or human resources. Under Causation Oriented, projects are demand-based or raw materials-based projects depending on the non-availability of certain goods or services; or the availability of certain raw materials, skill or other inputs as the dominant reason for starting the project. Under Magnitude Oriented, the size of investment forms the basis, projects may thus be classified as large-scale or small-scale depending upon the total project investment.

Techno-economic characteristics based classification is useful in facilitating the process of feasibility appraisal. United Nations and its specialized agencies use the International Standard Industrial classification for all economic activities (ISIC) in collection and compilation of economic data. Since this classification covers the entire field of human economic endeavor, it forms a useful basis for classification of projects.

Economic activities under this classification are grouped into ten divisions, which are subdivided into ninety sub-divisions. The broad groups are, *viz.* : Division '0' that comprises agriculture, forestry, hunting and fishing; Division '1' has mining and quarrying; Division '2' and '3' that includes manufacturing; Division '4' for construction; Division '5' that is electricity, gas, water and sanitary services; Division '6' that is commerce; Division '7' has transport, storage and communication; Division '8' that is services; and Division '9' are the activities which are not adequately described.

2

Project Management — An Overview

The basic building blocks of the traditional form of organization are a functional division of management and a well-defined hierarchical structure. Typically, a firm is organized into various departments such as production, purchasing, marketing, finance, personnel, engineering and research and development. Some of these departments have a line function and others have staff function. Line managers have the principal responsibility for achieving goals of the firm and are vested with decision making authority. Staff managers primarily serve in an advisory capacity of course, within the staff departments they enjoy administrative powers.

The traditional form of organization is quite appropriate for handling established operations which are characterized by continuous flow of repetitive work, with each department attending to its specific functions — in such setting, relatively stable inter-departmental and inter-personal relationships emerge. However, the traditional form of organization is not suitable for project management. There are several reasons :

1. A project is a non-routine, non-repetitive undertaking often plagued with many uncertainties.
2. The relationships in a project setting are dynamic, temporary and flexible.
3. A project requires coordination of efforts of persons drawn from different functional areas and contributions of external agencies.

Due to the above stated reasons, Project Management calls for a different form of organization, sharper tools of planning and control and improved means of coping with human problems. Therefore, the issues relating to Project Management can be divided into five sections, *viz.* : Forms of Project Organization, Project Planning, Project Control, Human Aspects of Project Management, and Pre-requisites for Successful Project Implementation.

I. Forms of Project Organization

The traditional form of organization is not suitable for project work for the following rationale : It has no means of integrating different departments at levels below the top management; and it does not facilitate effective communication, co-ordination and control, when several functional departments with different professional backgrounds and orientations are involved in project work under time and cost pressures, which often calls for overlap at atleast partial, of development, design, procurement, construction and commissioning work.

Hence there is a need for entrusting an individual (or group) with the responsibility for integrating the activities and functions of various departments and external organizations involved in the project work. Such an individual may be called the Project Manager. Depending on the authority that is given to the person responsible for the project, the Project Organization may take any of the following three forms : Line and Staff organization, Divisional organization or Matrix organization.

II. Project Planning

Projects involving few activities such as resources, constraints and inter-relationships can be visualized easily by human mind and planned informally. However, when a project crosses a certain threshold level of size and complexity, informal planning has to be substituted by formal planning. The need for formal planning is needed much greater for project work than for normal operations. Without effective planning, there may be CHAOS.

Planning is a vital aspect of management and it serves several important functions which include, providing a basis for organizing the work on the project and allocating responsibilities to individual; serves as a means of communication and coordination between all those involved in the project; induces people to look ahead; instills a sense of urgency and time consciousness; and establishes the basis for monitoring and control.

III. Project Control

No sooner is the project launched, control becomes the dominant concern of the Project Manager. Once the launch phase is over, planning and control become closely intertwined in an Integrated Managerial Process. Project Control involves a regular comparison of performance against targets, a search for the deviation and a commitment to check adverse variances. This function of Project Management serves two major functions, *viz.* : Ensures regular monitoring of performance; and it motivates project personnel to strive for achieving project objectives.

IV. Main Aspects of Project Management

A satisfactory Human Relations System is essential for the successful execution of a project. Without such a system, the other systems of Project Management, however sound they may be by themselves, are not likely to work well. While technical problems can be solved with additional investment of resources, people's problems may not be amenable to satisfactory solution in the short span of the Project Life.

To achieve satisfactory human relations in the project setting, the Project Manager must successfully handle problems and challenges relating to Authority, Orientation, Motivation and Group Functioning.

V. Prerequisites for Successful Project Implementation

Time and cost overruns of projects are very common in India, particularly in the public sector. An analysis of state projects would reveal similar picture. Due to such time and cost overruns, projects tend to become uneconomical, resources are not available to support other projects and economic development is adversely affected. What can be done to minimize time and cost overruns and thereby, improve the prospects of successful completion of projects.

While a lot of things can be done to achieve this goal, the more important one's appear to be the following : (a) Adequate Formulation, (b) Sound Project Organization, (c) Proper Implementation Planning, (d) Advance Action, (e) Timely Availability of Funds, (f) Judicious Equipment Tendering and Procurement, (g) Better Contract Management and (h) Effective Monitoring.

3

What is Project Management?

A good many people are involved in Project Management without knowing it. They can improve their performance by studying and applying the techniques of Project Management. The surveyor designing and producing maps of virgin territory and the site engineer in charge of a small building site are Project Managers, just as those who carry the title.

Who are Project Managers?

If we look at the description of Project Managers as people doing Project Management work, as written in some advertisements by consultant organizations and companies in media publications, this indicates the diversity of the term "Project Manager". Project Management, it can be concluded, is a comprehensive term, and can be applied by many people to many jobs, but there are many reasons for talking about it as Project Management, rather than just "Management".

When the task or job reaches such proportions of size or complexity that additional management is organized in lateral coordination, then "management" is usually termed as "Project Management". Its function is to drive the project forward as a project : Line management by definition must concern itself primarily with its line function tasks. The role of Project Manager thus, in the fullest sense would be as follows :

(a) To prepare and monitor the progress of the overall project plan in terms of cost, time, and function.

(b) To be the central authority for technical and management decisions on the project.

(c) To be responsible for the successful conclusion of the project in terms of cost, time, and function.

(d) To have equal influence with the line managers, in order to plan the use and allocation of resources.

(e) To be the reporting authority to the top management for the project.

Some companies are built around a series of large turnkey projects. These are : Atomic power establishments, oil exploration agencies, thermal power generation agencies, construction companies, among others. Project Management techniques are now extensively being used by the advanced technology manufacturing industry. The concept, Project Management evolves around two devices : A Management Arrangement and a System of Management Techniques.

Why is it a Project Management Arrangement?

It is to be observed that with the few function lines x (n), the coordination routes possible, and nearly always necessary, are n (n-1) = 12. In this case, where (n) is equal to the number of interrelating sections. (See Fig. 3.1) With this sort of quantity, the line managers would have difficulty in providing coordination. If the number of functional lines has grown, there is confusion of many function lines requiring inordinate amounts of line management work to get any project result at all. Consequently, there is no effective result towards the interfunctional goals. There is likely to be delay and possibility of high costs, together with a lack of success of the operation.

The great danger is that people furthest down the management chain, have no conception of the coordination required and those, further up the chain may realize it, but are too busy with line function to take note of it.

With a Project Management Arrangement, an effective control of the multi-threads of the vertical functional management can be exercised, from the project perspective as a technical skills' view-point. An illustration giving pictorial analogy to this control is depicted below in Fig. 3.2.

Whether or not the full organization and responsibilities of project management are effected in a company, the techniques

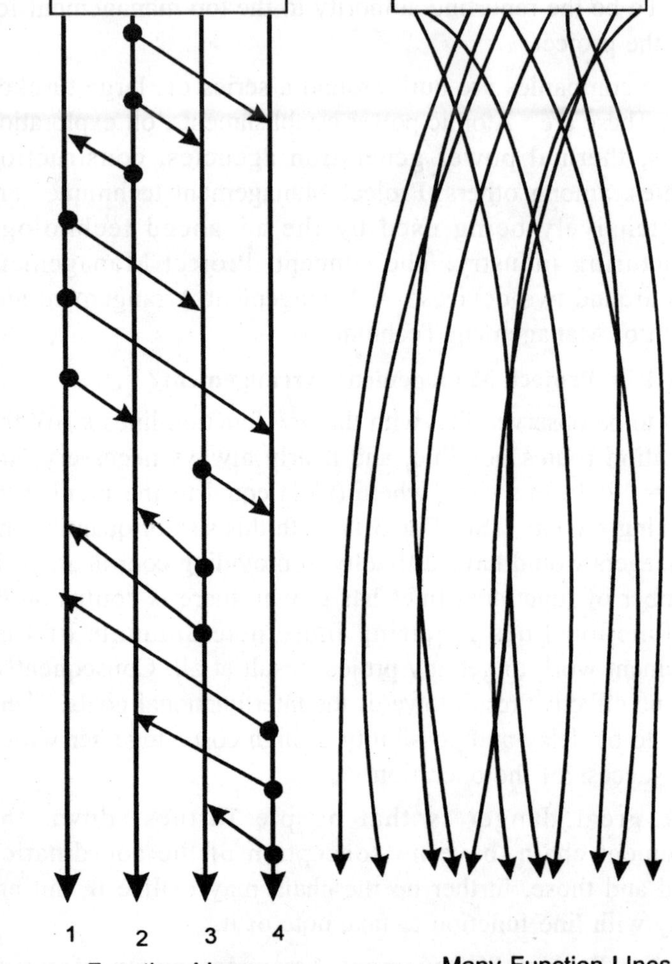

Fig. 3.1

that have grown up rapidly with project management can always be applied. These techniques ensure a practical approach to the management theory and philosophy and give a firm base for the advancement to higher grades of management.

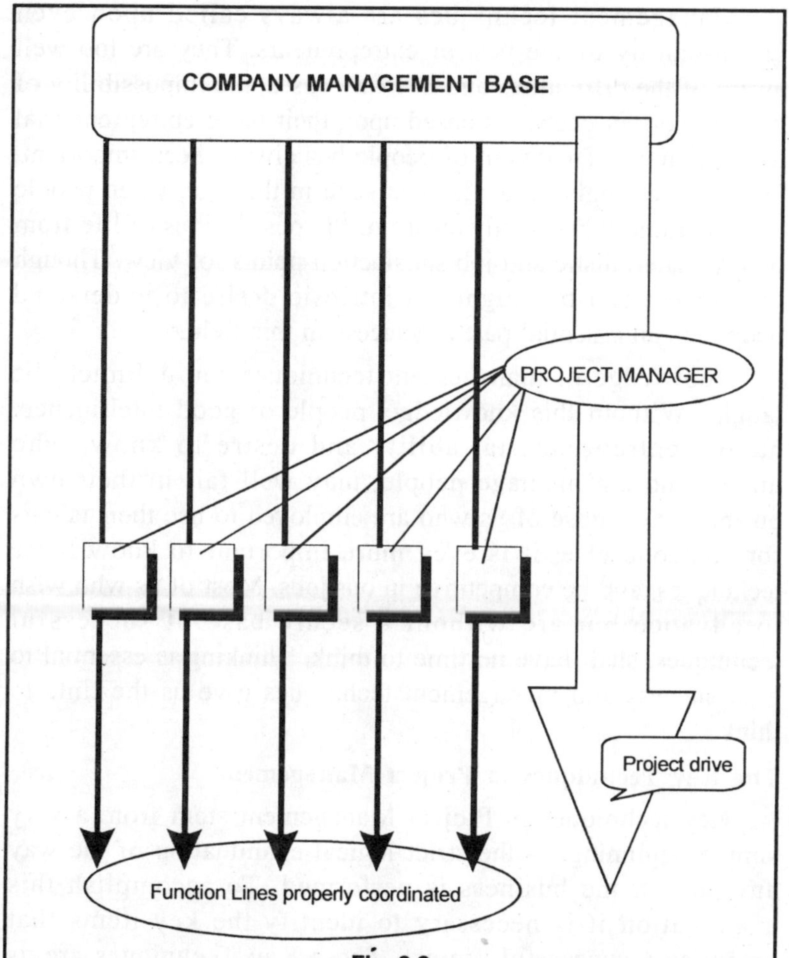

Fig. 3.2

In the management of all businesses, professions and small and large projects, there are three vital factors which bring success to an enterprise. These are as follows : (a) Basic entrepreneurial ability; (b) treatment of people; and (c) the knowledge of management techniques.The basic entrepreneurial ability can be taught but, more often than not, it is an innate sense; it includes a complete awareness of situations and the apparent ability to make more right decisions than wrong ones.

Management techniques are always called upon even unconsciously by the best of entrepreneurs. They are too well aware of the difficulties and in many cases, the impossibility of making correct decisions based upon their basic entrepreneurial abilities alone. Treatment of people has always been important, but is increasingly recognized as such in this age, when people are becoming increasingly aware of the possibilities of life from purely materialistic and job satisfaction points' of view. Though the subject can be taught, an intrinsic desire to understand people, is an essential part of success in this field.

Knowledge of management techniques can definitely be taught. Without this knowledge, people of good intelligence, having entrepreneurial ability and desire to know, who understand and manage people, may well fail in their own business. For those of us who are employed to use their talents for someone else, it is even more important to know these techniques, and be competitive in our jobs. Most of us who wish to advance but are without a secure base of successful techniques, shall have no time to think. Thinking is essential to plan success and management techniques give us the time to think.

The Key Techniques in Project Management

Key techniques in Project Management stem from a very simple beginning — the strict logical examination of the way any task in the business is performed. To accomplish this examination it is necessary to identify the key items that comprise a successful project. These Key Techniques are as mentioned below.

I. *Key Techniques No. 1 — Define The Task*

- What is the task?
- Describe it and identify it.
- Specify it in as much detailed a manner, as possible.
- Make sure that everybody who has to assist knows the task fully.

To define a task we must ask questions and receive answers, that fit in with other answers. We may have to guesstimate in some areas, as these may not be fully clear in the early stages. We have to have complete estimation that is enough to enable the committal of resources to occur with minimum risk. Taking full cognizance of the following paradigms regarding the general overall system and requirements are therefore required. Towards achieving this, a few questions need to be answered. We need to know : What are we trying to do or make? What are the principal functions? What are the existing special features? What are the new engineering or manufacturing processes available? Are there any new standards of quality and reliability? Are there any special time scales, prices, costs, risks, etc.?

In spite of all the care taken in defining the tasks, the definitions will change as we progress. Be prepared for changes that may be technology-related, or related to priority, requirements, business, etc.

II. *Key Technique No. 2 — Know What Total Resources are Required to Perform The Task*

This Key Technique entails inquiring questions not only about the resources available for the project in terms of finance, in terms of human effort—physical and mental, in terms of materials and equipment, in terms of space to perform the task and in terms of services; but also to ascertain whether these will be sufficient to perform the project task. To accomplish this, it is essential to understand the scope of the lexicon used :

- Finance implies provision for budgets, cash flow and risk analyses.
- Human effort must be in terms of type, grade, ability, and suitability. It also includes supervision and management types.
- Materials would mean special raw materials, plant, equipment and consumables.
- Space would mean land, buildings, warehouses, roads and offices.

- Services would include electric power, compressed air, water — industrial as well as potable.

Decisions made about resources must be consonant with time-scales, quality, reliability, costs of production and product costs. As the project progresses, unforeseen delays are bound to occur regularly causing project gestation.

III. *Key Technique No. 3 — Know The Time-scales in Terms of all Activities, Events and Resources*

In order to avoid project gestation, knowing the time-scales is a key technique in Project Management. Time-scales must be translated in terms of when to obtain the resources, as well as when to employ and apply those resources.

If the time-scale is already specified, the resources must be chosen to meet an acceptable, economical and viable time-table. The earlier a project is completed, the greater is its marketability power. Shorter time-scales without accompanying "crash" costs enabling earlier sales give better cash flow returns on the investment. In the building up of a complete time plan for a project, a considerable number of activities will emerge. It will be advantageous to thoroughly examine the logic, as well as activity times.

IV. *Key Technique No. 4 — What Quality and Reliability is to be Achieved*

The quality and reliability objectives may be already specified, in which case the resources and time-scales have to be suitably adjusted. If these are not already specified, a decision has to be made as to what standards the quality and reliability shall be. In case these are not detailed at all, there is always a possibility of the following repercussions : Time-scales will change; resources will change and therefore, costs will have to change.

However, with modern technology and value control techniques, quality and reliability can be obtained at no extra cost, in some cases at less cost. This would mean looking for newer technologies, looking for the "best" value and using value analysis.

V. *Key Technique No. 5 — Know your Product Cost*

The product's price may be set after the establishment of costs or by other considerations like marketing or both. Notwithstanding the above, do not economize on critical path items that are a small part of the total cost or where the number of items make an amortized increase in the cost, each of which is a small percentage of the original cost.

Watch quality, reliability and function when cost reductions are being planned. Until the product cost is known in absolute detail, part-by-part, function-by-function and within the proper overheads by cost centers, effective cost design is not possible. In this scenario, it is essential to press the organization for more efficient, fast, and accurate costing.

VI. *Key Technique No. 6 — Make a Continuous, Conscious and Disciplined Approach to Optimize The Value*

Value must always be, in part, intangible. There are however, other aspects of the value question in terms of the tangible items. Therefore it is required that you seek an answer to the question : Is the cost, time, quality and success of function relationship in proper balance?

Since "value" is optimum when the "function" is obtained at the lowest cost with an acceptable time-scale and quality, the use of value analysis or value engineering proves good.

Get the best value from bought out materials and finished goods, not by beating down your subcontractors by bringing them into your value optimization schemes. Let them be competitive and make a profit. Profit is the motive for business. Value means profit for everybody, the customer included. If the customer gets value, this attracts more business, hence more profit.

VII. *Key Technique No. 7 — Measure the Project Performance*

This key technique entails measuring the project performance continually with adequate control and taking up corrective measures wherever needed. Ensure that the top management is kept informed about the project status on a continual basis and watch out for top-level key events. These are the jumping off platforms to the next major activity. Keep it in mind to measure the performance of everything affecting the project : subcontractors, all company personnel who are contributing and customer contributions, especially in terms of premises, payments, etc.

The Systems' Or Operations' Management Approach

Refer to the Project Management process with key techniques noted against the items in the illustration given below in Fig. 3.3. The illustration shows clearly that there is little independence among the key techniques. For example, if the resources are increased without high quality or increased specification of the task then the value per unit falls. This may show an effect on the time-scale as well.

This inter-dependence upon one another puts the key techniques into a unique position — they form a system of actions; and one key technique is not altered without knowing the effect on one or more of the others. This is what makes the successful Project Management different from an inexperienced approach. Successful Project Management is an integrated systems' approach to the project with the awareness of all the key techniques and their influence on one another. To get out of the vicious circle of recurring crisis, the outcome of unplanned approach requires effort on the part of the persons' responsible, over and above the daily routine, until the correct plans are laid to stop the crisis of "tomorrow".

The plan that will be derived, if we use all the Project Management techniques, as detailed in this book will be a good one. It will stand up to all the tests that the top management can give it, but, no plan can remain rigid forever. Plans have to change in the light of information feedback, starting from the execution of those plans. The project will not run itself, however good it may be. Progress measurement in as much depth as possible must be carried out, all the time to anticipate potential problems.

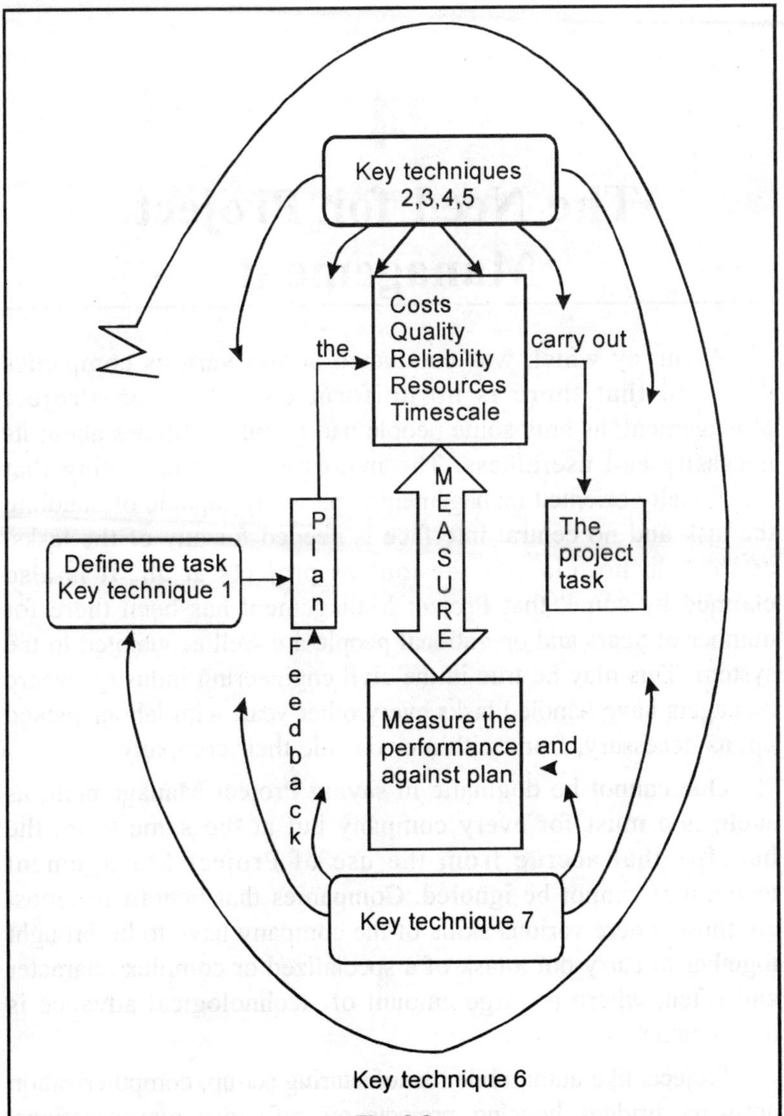

Fig. 3.3

SYSTEM APPROACH

4

The Need for Project Management

A survey which was conducted across various companies revealed that there is no uniform consensus on Project Management; as only some people had definite attitudes about its necessity and usefulness. The majority have the feeling that functionally oriented management is perfectly capable of handling the task and no central interface is needed for any of the tasks, as they do not classify the jobs as projects at all. It is also claimed by some, that Project Management has been there for number of years and operational people are well acquainted to the system. This may be true in the civil engineering industry, where managers have handled tasks every other year, with labour picked up, as necessary, from within or outside their company.

One cannot be dogmatic in saying Project Management, as such, is a must for every company but at the same time, the benefits that accrue from the use of Project Management techniques cannot be ignored. Companies that benefit the most are those where various skills of the company have to be brought together to carry out a task of a specialized or complex character and often, where a large amount of technological advance is being made.

Projects like automobile manufacturing set-up, computerization net-work, bridges, housing projects, oil refineries, power stations, railways and the like, which require high degree of co-ordination, involving many divisions within the company and outside contractors, demand a common technical and managerial interface and thus the one person to look after them is a Project Manager.

Organizations are groups of people and facilities set up within a company to perform single or multiple tasks. The need to divide the company into organizations (groups, divisions and sections) arise from a desire to - put like operations in one compartment or keep unlike operations such as sales, R & D, production, purchase and accounting, separate.

This arrangement has obvious advantages, as different skills are grouped together for better overall control. However, the disadvantage is typical of functionally oriented organization where the overall co-ordination can vest only with the Managing Director of the company. Immediately below him, there is no one in authority to deal effectively and rapidly with project problems. In such a situation there is a need for cross-functional coordination.

The usual remedy for project problems is to set up a committee to deal with it. By and large, these committees are found to be ineffective simply because the members are not fully aware of their authority or their real function.

If the project is complex, organizationally, technically or financially large, then a central technical and managerial interface must be created, that is a Project Management organization and a Project Manager. A project needs nurture and drive, as well as application of all the Project Management key techniques.

A simple example of the interaction of project parts at various stages of their life cycle and the need for Project Management is say, construction of a large block of flats. In the office of main contractor, the preliminary work is carried out on drawings, plans, costs, specifications and appropriate time-scales in order that the various planning permissions can be obtained. When it is clear that the project can proceed, detailed plans of all activities must be made, dovetailing the activities of all types of skills to ensure that the project finishes on time and at correct cost.

Several subcontractors are also engaged, apart from the main contractor, on items such as : Precast concrete blocks and slabs, steel construction, ventilation, flooring, plastering, roof glazing, etc.

The subcontract orders and timing together with ordering of material to arrive at planned times, must be achieved. When the project commences, the site can be cleared and foundation concrete started. Whenever any complications arise someone at the site can judge and take appropriate action. For example, regarding the site clearance, it can be ascertained whether it is started and if it is ready for the excavators? If the activity has not proceeded, it is necessary to decide what course of action must be taken. Again, when the site is cleared, it may be verified whether the foundation digging has commenced? Or whether the machinery is at the site? Whether the plans are understood properly, etc.?

Normally at the project site, a Site Engineer or a Project Manager is responsible to ensure that the job proceeds smoothly and it is he who has to take corrective action whenever needed for smooth work.

Difficulties of Project Management

There are three main difficulties in the area of Project Management. Two of these difficulties concern the work content itself. The first is related to the technical difficulties and external factors, such as material deliveries or subcontractors' labour; and second concern is the management's attitude at various levels towards the Project Manager.

It is generally acknowledged that function oriented structure is superior in say design, production engineering, manufacturing, etc. The managers of these functions are jealous and often resent any attempt at coordination across these functions. The resentment is usually manifested in the form of lack of cooperation with the Project Manager or his staff. A typical example of this can be the case of a design passing into manufacture. This interface can be difficult as decisions taken by either one are based on different views. Therefore the design engineers should work closely with production. It is here that a Project Manager can, and certainly has to, exercise his diplomacy and technical skill to ensure a smooth passage of design to production.

To sum up, an important difficulty of application of Project Management is the non-acceptance by the line function of the company, who believe that labour division by skills and their own infallibility, will be sufficient. It is only when a complex project is conceived for execution, that the top management pins responsibility on the head of its favorite manager. It is a fact, that mediocre Project Management may be better than none at all, so that the job looks like a success. It also seems a foregone conclusion that as the technological complexity grows, project management will become increasingly necessary.

5

The Project Manager and His Place in the Organization

The success of the project depends on the abilities and character of the Project Manager. He must command respect and be able to secure the cooperation of line managers in his own company, as well as contractors, customers and staff members. The Project Manager must have a clear place in the company's management hierarchy. He must have the knack of getting along with people. He must be able to freely communicate with a wide variety of people. He is essentially a practical man and must find his way around overcoming the problems. He needs to have some technical knowledge pertaining to the project under consideration. At the same time, the bulk of his experience needs to be management oriented. He has to use his knowledge of Project Management techniques to achieve results.

Projects can involve many different disciplines and specializations. It is important that he is professionally knowledgeable, in some of these areas. He must have the ability to realize the need for expert advice and help in other areas. One of the most important responsibilities of the Project Manager is to ensure that all parties contributing to the project have a clear and unambiguous understanding of the project, its aim and the purpose. He must make sure that each party's understanding is the alike. This requires an ability to think logically and communicate effectively.

The Project Manager is a planner, manager and persuader. He must be capable of managing other people. He must have a logical mind to be able to plan and carry out key techniques in a methodical and organized way. A lot of work of the project is done through line managers of other departments of the company and lots of subcontractor firms. He must be able to persuade them to do what is required for the success of the project. The Project Manager must appreciate the importance of his project and his seniors in the management hierarchy need to back him, in enforcing the cooperation of the line managers.

The size of a project will affect the seniority and the type of Project Manager that is selected. Two main elements of a project determine its size. These are the complexity of the project and the risk involved. Where there is no complexity and no risk, there is no need for a Project Manager. A project breaks down into a number of activities. Complexity can arise because of the number and diversity of these activities and its interdependence on each other. These contributory factors include the number of different divisions of the company which are involved; the number of external parties such as subcontractors, suppliers, government regulatory bodies etc.; and the inclusion of items that are still under development.

Even small items "to be developed" can add considerably to the complexity of the project. The size or importance of a project depends on the risks involved. The risks arise from the following factors :

(a) Almost everything that leads to complexity in a project, also leads to risk.

(b) The extent to which future business and profits depend upon the success of this project.

(c) The likely consequences of failing to meet project completion dates at specified performance levels and within budgeted costs.

(d) The tightness of the contract, on which the project is based.

(e) The more new elements there are in a project, the greater is the risk involved.

The Project Manager must be totally dedicated to the success of the project. He must be a forceful and determined leader, who is not deterred by minor setbacks. He must see the problems as issues that are to be solved and not as excuses for failure. He must be able to communicate his ideas clearly to other people, depicting his sincerity and enthusiasm. The Project Manager needs to know who the right people are, and know them well. The priority that a company gives to a project is important. A Project Manager has to face two main issues : The struggle against internal project problems; and to obtain the priority he needs for his work within the company. He will face constant competition for priority from the normal line functions.

The structure of Project Management varies from company to company. It is not just the organization chart that matters. It is the way it works in practice that is important. Let us examine the following organization structures.

Fig. 5.1 is a typical of many small-to-medium sized companies, based on line function. If the projects are concerned with the

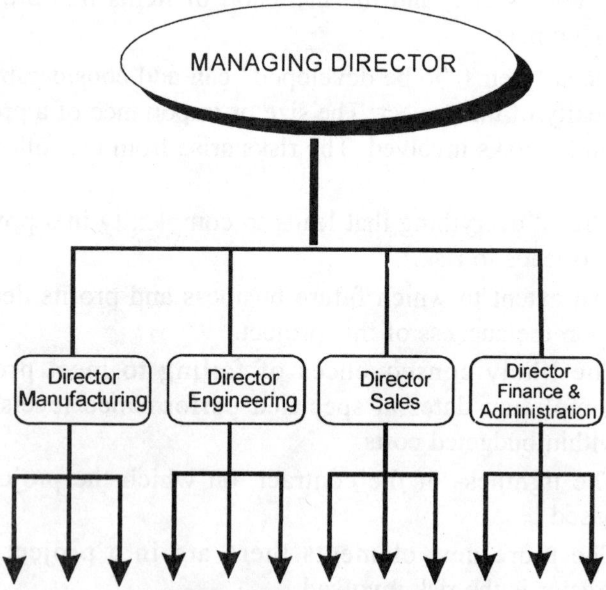

Fig. 5.1. FUNCTION LINE STRUCTURE

development of new products, they might be placed under the engineering, as shown in Fig. 5.2. Where the project entails large proportions of size or complexity which requires extensive coordination with various agencies, the Project Management is an independent function, may be, reporting to the Managing Director as shown in Fig. 5.3 below.

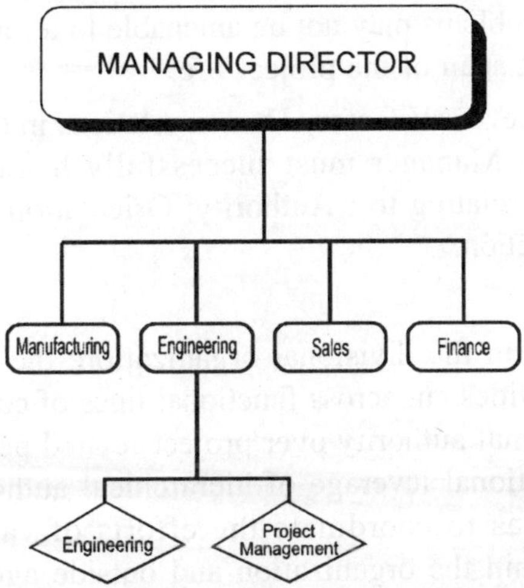

Fig. 5.2. PROJECT MANAGEMENT BY LINE FUNCTION

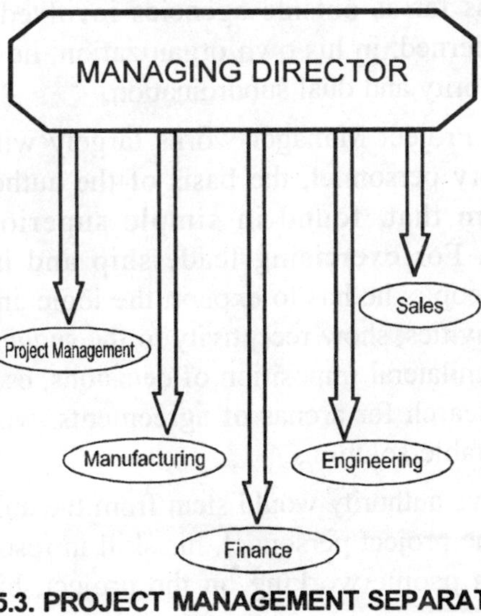

Fig. 5.3. PROJECT MANAGEMENT SEPARATE

Human Aspects of Project Management

A satisfactory Human Relations system is essential for successful execution of a project. Without such a system, the other Systems Project Management, however sound they may be by themselves, are not likely to work well. While typical problems can often be solved with additional investment of resources, people's problems may not be amenable to a satisfactory solution in the short span of the project life.

To achieve satisfactory Human relations in the project setting, the Project Manager must successfully handle problems and challenges relating to : Authority; Orientation; Motivation; and Group Function.

Authority

Except in the divisional organization, the Project Manager whose activities cut across functional lines of command lacks the desired formal authority over project-related personnel. Without the conventional leverage of hierarchical authority, the Project Manager has to coordinate the efforts of various functional groups within the organization and outside agencies. While he often has formal control emanating from contracts and agreements, as far as outside agencies involved in the project work are concerned, in his own organization, he has to contend with split authority and dual subordination.

Since the Project Manager works largely with professional and supervisory personnel, the basis of the authority would be different from that, found in simple superior-subordinate relationships. For exercising leadership and influence over professional people, he has to explain the logic and rationale for the project activities, show receptivity to the suggestions made by others, avoid unilateral imposition of decisions, eschew dogmatic postures and search for arenas of agreements, which can be the basis of acceptable solutions.

His effective authority would stem from the ability to develop rapport with the project personnel, his skill in resolving conflicts among various people working on the project, his professional reputation and stature, his skill in communication and persuasion and his ability to act as a buffer between the technical engineering, financial and commercial people involved in the project.

Orientation

Most of the managers who work for a project are usually engineers or technologists. Typically, an engineer will work with physical laws characterized by mathematical precision as his tools. He must adopt a structured, mechanical approach to his problems; seek an enduring solution to his problems and attach a high value on technical perfection. When an engineer assumes managerial responsibilities, he faces a very different world in which he is supposed to perform the tasks of planning, organizing, directing and controlling the resources of the firm in a world of uncertainty. He has to adopt a more creative approach to solve non-programme and unstructured problems. He has to also attach greater importance to efficient utilization of resources and resolution of Human Relation problems.

Thus, the Project Manager has to strengthen the managerial orientation of project personnel, so that the project goals and objectives can be efficiently achieved within the constraints of time and budget.

Motivation

The Project Manager functions within the boundaries of a socio-technical system. Most of the factors of this system-organizational structure, technical requirements, competencies of project personnel — are more or less "specified" for him. The principal behavioral factor that can influence here, is the motivation of the project personnel. In this context, he should bear in mind the following perspectives :

Human beings are motivated be variety of needs, *viz.* : Psychological needs, social needs, recognition needs and self-actualization needs. Individuals differ greatly in the importance they attach to various need satisfactions. Further, their attitudes tend to change with time and circumstances and are influenced by their peers and superiors

The traditional approach to management was based on the assumption that human beings regard work as unpleasant, shirk responsibility and ordinarily employ inefficient, wasteful methods. Such a conception of human behaviour suggests that a great deal of pressure needs to be applied in completion of a task. Behavioural research however, has shown that while some pressure is beneficial, an excess of it is undesirable. Beyond a certain point, pressure can be dysfunctional.

Motivation tends to be strong when the goal set is challenging, yet attainable. If the goal is too demanding, it results in frustration and conflict, if too lax, it induces complacency. Expectation or reward, rather than fear of punishment has a greater bearing on individual behaviour. Further, the effectiveness of reward or punishment depends on how quickly it is administered. In a project setting where hygiene factors like pay, physical working conditions, etc., are reasonably taken care of, the principal motivators would be a sense of accomplishment and professional growth. In this setting, the Project Manager should rely more on participative method of management. In order to succeed in motivating project personnel, the Project Manager must be a perceptive observer of human beings. He must have the ability to appreciate the variable needs of human beings; he must have skill in several styles of management suitable to different situations and must be sensitive to reactions of people so that he can act supportively rather than threateningly.

Understandably, the Project Manager has a difficult task. In this endeavor he can however, count on one blessing : The stimulating and satisfying nature of the project work. In established organizations, many professional and supervisory personnel find it difficult to see, how their efforts lead to the realization of organizational goals. Separated from the top management be several layers of organizational hierarchy, they are unable to relate their work to the missions of the firm. In addition, the jobs in established organizations are somewhat dull and routine. All this creates a sense of alienation and frustration, which dampens motivation.

Fortunately, in a project setting, where subordinate goals are clearly defined and visible to all involved, where there is usually a great emphasis on participative style of management, where the layers in the organizational hierarchy are few and where the jobs are more challenging, project personnel tend to have greater commitment. Being able to relate their work easily to the goals of the project, their motivation is usually high.

Group Function

In a large and complex project, many persons drawn from different functions, departments and organizations are involved. This leads to formation of Groups — formal and informal. According to Rensis Likert, organizations may be considered as systems of interlocking and interdependent groups. The group formed in a project setting may be any of the three types, namely : Vertical groups, horizontal groups and mixed groups.

(i) *A Vertical Group* consists of people drawn from different levels in the same department or function or company.

(ii) *A Horizontal Group* consists of people drawn from different functions, departments and companies, but occupying similar hierarchical positions.

(iii) *A Mixed Group* consists of people drawn from different levels from various functions, departments and companies.

A vertical group tends to form more naturally, because of departmental/functional/organizational affinities. However, the existence of such a group, may lead to a pronounced "we/they" attitude and accentuated conflicts. A horizontal group, on the other hand, is a useful instrument in linking the overall project organization, wherein the group members occupying key positions in their respective fields, serve as channels of communication. By their influence, they can strengthen the commitment to the project.

The mixed group tends to promote greater cohesion of the total project organization. It is very conducive in creating a "project attitude" and developing an overriding commitment to the project. Hence the Project Manager should strive to establish a mixed group as the principal group of the project. However this may be difficult, because of the temporary nature of a project — when the members of a group know that the group would be dissolved sooner or later, they retain strong links with their parent company or department.

Building Effective Groups

Groups therefore consists members who are satisfied and committed and who strive for the attainment of project objectives, without dissipating their energies in interpersonal and intergroup conflicts. The manifest signs are : Esprit de corps, pride in the project, supportive behaviour, coordinated endeavour, mutual respect and resilience during trying periods. An Effective Group members who are more involved in interpersonal and intergroup rivalries and less concerned about project goals. Such a group is characterized by apathy, animosity, mutual bickering, disjointed efforts, cynical attitudes and low morale.

How can an Effective Group be established? Studies in group dynamics suggest several stages, which are partially overlapping in the formation of an effective group :

(a) Development of mutual trust.

(b) Diminution of defensive behaviour.

(c) Openness and candor in communication.

(d) Cooperation and supportive behaviour.

(e) Resolution of differences by mutual negotiation.

For building an Effective group, the firm must pursue a genuinely participative style of management. With this managerial philosophy, the Project Manager can facilitate the development of mutual trust and acceptance, open communication, cooperation and project attitude. In this task, he needs leadership capabilities, sensitivity to human nature, perceptiveness, concern for welfare of others maturity and impartial approach.

6

Defining the Project

Two of the prime requirements of good management are the ability and the will to plan. It is absolutely essential to plan the work in the minutest detail. This plan must start with *Key Technique No. 1*, that is a proper identification of the task. It is of prime importance for the Project Manager to know what job he has to manage. There are always a multitude of questions that cannot be addressed in the early stages of the project.

On the basis of information inputs from Marketing and R & D departments, a feasibility report prepared by corporate planning is discussed in the meeting of the Company's Board of Directors. If the company's board agrees with the evaluation of the feasibility study, then the Project Manager is called upon hereafter to carry out a Detailed Project Report (DPR) of the project.

For the preparation of DPR, the Project Manager consults functional managers and experts to gather relevant information to compile the report. Reports of this nature consist of a summary in which all the key information is presented in the form of a written report. The report shall invariably include financial analysis, discounted cash flow and project gestation time in detail. The whole aim is to identify the task in order that the management may know clearly what risks are involved and what rewards can be expected. The whole project report and subsequent reports should follow the principles of project identification triangle, as illustrated in Fig. 6.1. The essence of all

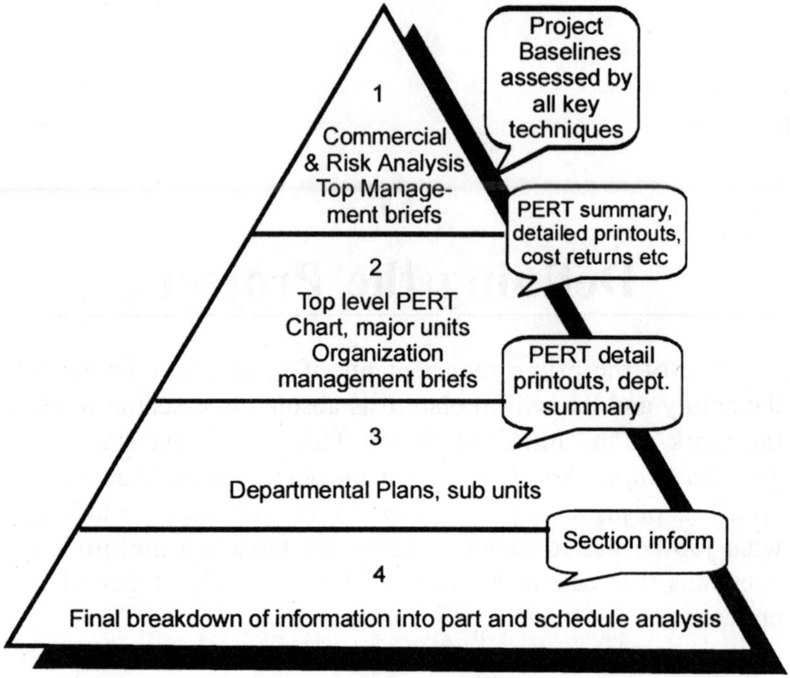

Fig. 6.1

THE PROJECT IDENTIFICATION TRIANGLE

identification is the break-down of work into dimensions : The time it takes, the resources needed, its place in the total specification hierarchy, etc. However, as is normal with any project, full details are never available until the project progresses.

In any project, while there are multitude of activities comprising the total effort, there are in general only a few top level objectives which when defined or specified correctly, set the scene of the project. These can be elucidated as follows :

The System Concept comprising of system feasibility, concept feasibility, system aim, project aim, project formulation, etc.

The Project Definition comprising of system definition, project specifications., job specifications, etc.

Design and Development encompassing engineering, design and drawing, engineering developments, etc.

Manufacturing encompassing all aspects of pre-production to full-production.

Field Usage comprising all aspects of customer operations.

In each of the above stated objectives, there has to be a fully defined and measurable specification; without which, control is not possible and the project could easily slip to disaster.

The System Concept would mean : A full description of what we are trying to accomplish; a full assessment of how we are going to achieve the task — the research, the technical approach and the technology required; a full examination of time-scales and lower level key objectives; complete cost estimates; and definition of all resources — human support and material support — including the management of the project.

The Project Definition would mean : A full specification of the project including separate specifications for major units, especially for items bought from outside (specifications include drawings, sketches, etc. that will help specify the product).

The Design and Development would mean : Building of prototypes; and proving of prototypes to the full specification now evolved, a design review, feasibility of manufacturing the product and design changes, if necessary.

Manufacturing would mean : Proving of production engineering; and proving product cost, and design changes, if necessary.

Field Usage would mean: Review of field report on breakdowns and performance; and statistical work by quality assurance and design changes, if necessary.

A common pattern applicable to all projects is a three dimensional picture of the project drive to fruition. The first dimension is the project thrust through the key objectives; the second one is the application of all key objectives; and the third one, is the line function skills applicable and measured by the key techniques.

7

Getting Down to Business

In Chapter Six, we have established the major headings of a business plan, as well as a detailed definition of the new product. The Project Manager was authorized to get the task started in a proper manner. Very often, the Project Manager is brought in too late, after many crucial decisions have already been taken; however, this does not happen in those enlightened companies who use Project Management properly.

Initial Organization

An organization must be set up appropriate to the size of the project; many projects will involve perhaps only the Project Manager and a Secretary as "the Project Management". Others may involve a Project Management team, the Project Manager, the Secretary and key assistant managers. This very much depends on the interpretation of the picture presented to the top management by the facts as known, as depicted by the illustration given in Fig. 7.1 given here.

The Essential Steps

Key Technique No. 1 — Define The Task

Though we have defined the task and written a detailed report in chapter six, that was before the Project Management organization was put in place. The first task for the Project Manager is to talk with the managers and appropriate staff, selected for this purpose, in order to discuss thoroughly the project definition and make the job clear to all. In these discussions, the next key techniques also need to be taken up.

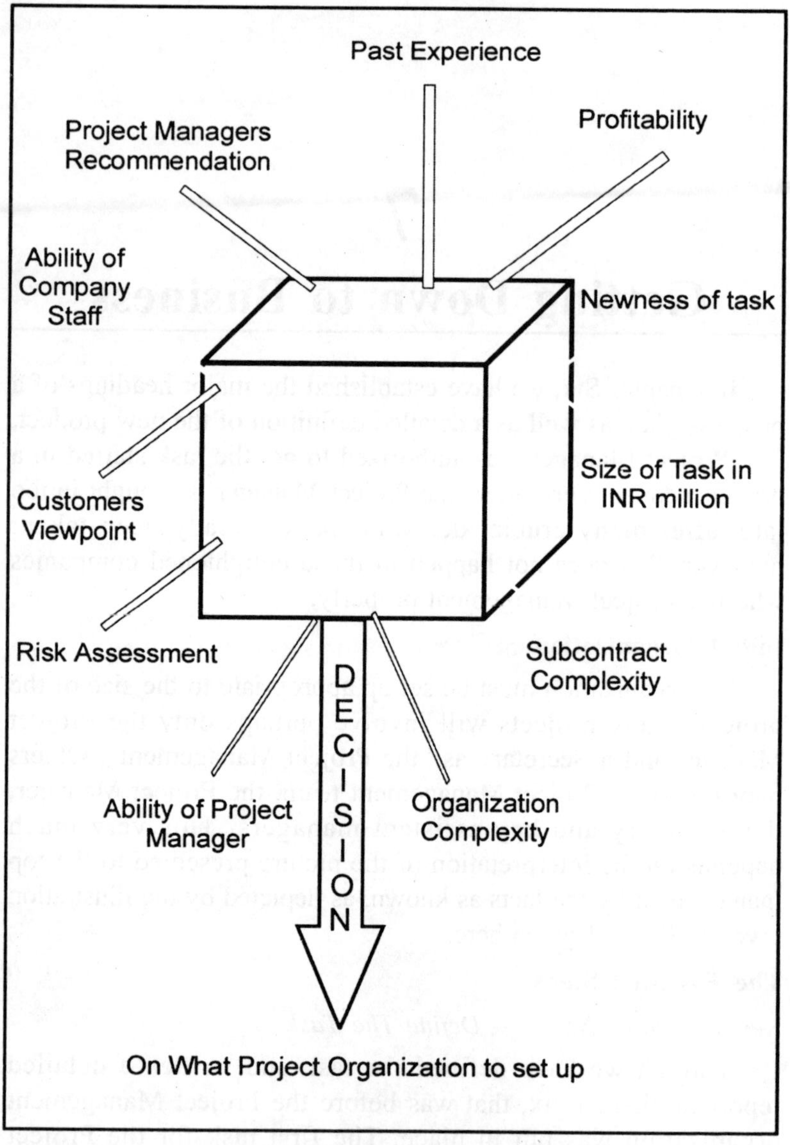

Fig. 7.1

DETERMINATION OF PROJECT ORGANISATION

Key Technique No. 2 — Resources

This can be bifurcated into the five relevant areas as detailed below :

(i) Finance. Notwithstanding the business plan report, budgets must now be assessed in the light of the most up-to-date information compiled based on the assumed feasible time-scale. Through the proper management chain, the comprehensive budget thus prepared, must be got approved by the Managing Director and the project is then "legal". This budget must distinctly reflect the existence of long-term and short-term budgets. The Project Manager should ensure that the Accounts Department prepares an overall project budget and expenditure summary as a control account.

In the budgeting will be included the result of examining the other facets of *Key Technique No. 2*, that is manpower, materials, equipment, space and services. There will be, as subsidiary to the main cash flow of the project as a whole, sub-cash flows to justify, say, this or that type of equipment. Like all the project processes, the concept of equipment comes first, with costs as revealed in the concept stage. As the project passes to the specification stage and beyond, a closer look can be taken at all the costs. Budgeting and cost justifications must be a continuous process to optimize the value of the project.

Some of the examples of budgeting formats are depicted below for guidance in tables (Refer to Table 7.2 and Table 7.3).

SHORT TITLE OF WORK

Labour & Overheads	Years 1		Total	Project Type
	1	2		
Workshop Sheet Metal Design Purchase Subcontract				Project Development Product Improvement Research & Techniques Project Number

Fig. 7.2. EXAMPLE OF BUDGET APPLICATION

PROJECT TITLE OF WORK

	Expenditure Type	Budget	Expense	Variance
Quality	Planning			
	Product approval Tests			
Manufacturing	Development Planning Introduction costs Product service			
Project Management	Manpower Other costs			
Engineering	Development Prototype build			
Others				
Total				

Fig. 7.3. EXAMPLE OF SUMMARY EXPENSE REVIEW

(ii) Manpower. The manpower budget applies itself to types of people who must be involved, for example, the specialists in any area, the supervisors and the managers. It should clearly show the build-up of staff on this project and effects on other projects, if run simultaneously in the assumed time-scale. (Refer to Table 7.4).

	MONTH								
Type	1	2	3	4	5	6	7	8	9
Prototype									
Engineering									
Production									
Finance									
Purchase									
Marketing									
Project Management									
Total									

Fig. 7.4. MANPOWER LIST

In compiling this listing, adequate precautions need to be exercised to avoid calamitous financial effects. To recruit a man is fairly easy, but to ensure he is the right man is difficult, to train him in a short time is even more difficult. Even with skilled and experienced personnel it may be several months before they are really functioning at top efficiency.

(iii) Materials and Equipment. We should have to define the materials and equipment types, costs and arrival times. In terms of materials, the first risks may now have to be assumed. Until now, no actual cash has been spent, except on the feasibility report and budget preparation. To a large extent, these are "overhead" items and will occur inside the company again. The Project Manager must, after careful examination of the detailed plans prepared, sanction the ordering of any long overdue delivery items. The risk is twofold. The financial risk in the sense that the wrong materials may prove to have been ordered in light of subsequent experience and secondly, that time may be wasted in procuring correct materials if a mistake has been made. Ordering is dictated by the time-scale, the money involved and the possible risks. Materials will include both raw materials and partly finished or fully finished items.

In terms of equipment, the risk element is similar to that of materials. The time-scale will decide the ordering time. Equipment will cover special equipment for early engineering development, manufacturing process development or test equipment development. While examining the necessity for such orders it is essential to have the time-scale and logic of the plan thoroughly vetted as there is no point in buying materials and equipment before it is absolutely necessary. The effects of not ordering must be well known. There may be a way around the problem until the Project Manager is more certain of the items he requires. The cost of waste on the other hand may be less than the cost of delays.

A careful record must be kept of material expenditure and a simple budget and expenditure chart (like the one shown in Fig. 7.5) will suffice. Graphical information can be maintained similar to the capital budget records for equipment. (Please refer to Fig. 7.6).

Project		Project No.	
Budget Rs.		Class of Materials	
Date	Item brought	Amount	Balance

Fig. 7.5. MATERIAL CONTROL FORM

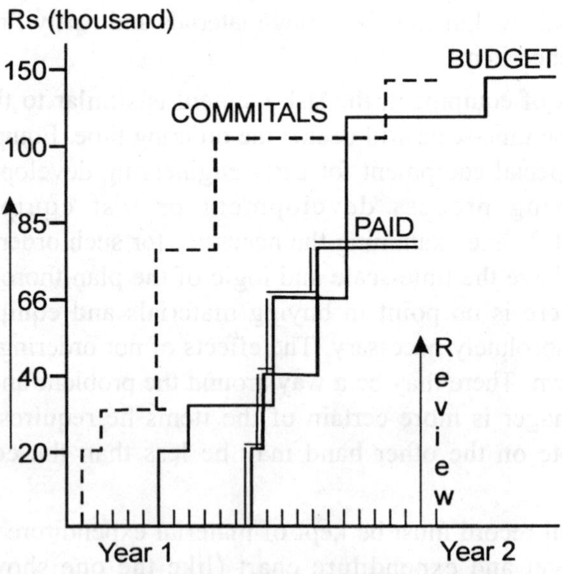

FIG. 7.6. CAPITAL CONTROL GRAPH

(iv) Capital Budget. Since capital is treated very differently from revenue in company accounts, it is necessary to log it separately. Apart from capital expenditure approvals and records, it is useful to have a capital budget and expenditure graph as illustrated in Fig. 7.6. On this graph can also be put committed figures because often an order for capital equipment is placed many months ahead. If a project has to be closed down, it is essential to know what is committed as well as what is actually paid for. If the plant on order is required to be cancelled, cancellation charges will have to be borne.

(v) Space. The effects of the project may mean no changes in the provision of overall space or it may mean new buildings, warehouses or extensions of existing facilities. Space requirement is a function of the added plant and equipment, manufacturing lines, welfare facilities and the like. Adequate knowledge of these items must be available before space requirements can be properly calculated. The main function of Project Manager is again to consult the line managers who are aware of the project's likely demand. Space could also be required for warehousing for the site contractors' tools and tackles, materials as well the pre-erection preparation activity.

(vi) Services and Facilities. The normal facilities of electricity, gas and water are fairly straight forward, at least in terms of engineering factories; the complications set in for chemical factories or metal processing plants. However, in the event project demands exceed by big margins, then these need to be considered afresh or may call for drastic changes in its distribution networks and the like. It may, in worst cases, require the upgrading of high tension feeder lines, high tension transformer yard, captive generation station, compressor bank, underground/overhead water storage facilities and connecting distribution networking. Notwithstanding the increased scope of the task, the key techniques shall cover all instances.

Key Technique No. 3 — Time-scales

In fact, *Key Technique No. 2 and Key Technique No. 3* are so interdependent that, at times, these can be combined together. Firstly, a time plan must be drawn up, using PERT methods. It is necessary that the key event dates are circulated to the line managers, to enable them to prepare detailed plans of their activities together, with reasons for any divergence from the key plan. The Key Plan can be simply a list of dates (as depicted in Fig.7.7) or a line plan as illustrated below in Fig. 7.8.

Event or Activity	Start Date	Finish Date	Duration	Level of Item

Fig. 7.7. EXAMPLE OF LIST OF KEY EVENTS

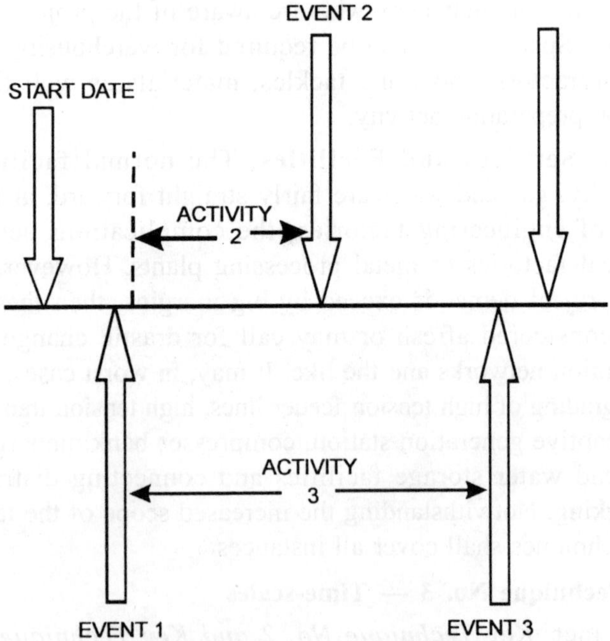

Fig. 7.8. LINE OF KEY EVENTS

During this process, the Project Manager will be spending much of his time with the appropriate staff, who are drawing up the plans. The Project Manager must not influence their decisions at this stage, but make sure there is no doubt in anybody's mind, as to what the project task really is. The plans of all departments will get integrated in time for revisions and approval by the Project Manager and top management. If PERT is used in conjunction with the computer, all the departmental groups of activities are obtainable quite simply as print-outs.

The complete logic of the plan must be checked and agreed with all the responsible managers. As a matter of urgency after that the complete plan, must be computer run to give all dates in a tabulated form. The key dates must be separately extracted from the PERT process. That the plans can be integrated will guarantee in itself, that there is no separation of functional organization. Please refer to Fig. 7.9 in this connection.

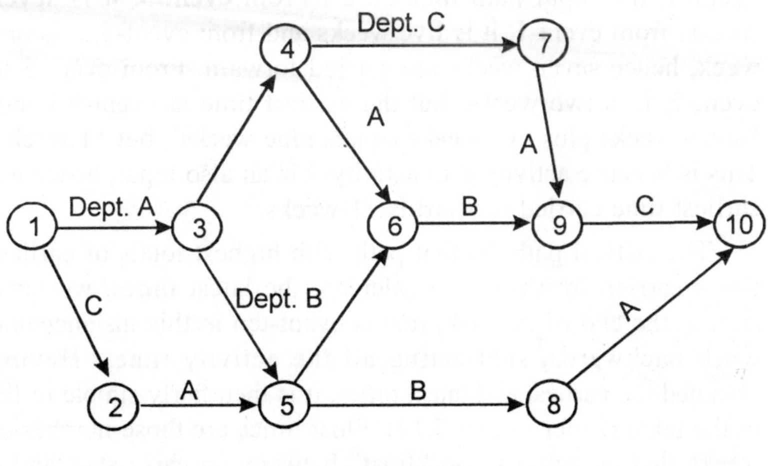

Fig. 7.9
EXAMPLE OF PERT CHART

At this stage of the project, speed is essential in feeding back the appropriate information to organization and departmental managers, because it is certain that the time-scales will not be in harmony. This "round the course" action may have to be carried out two or three times, until all line management, top management and project management are in unison and are convinced, that they have a feasible risk plan laid down within the budgets.

The Interplay Between Time-scales and Resources

Fig. 7.10 shows a network illustration for the installation of a heating system. Figures in brackets after the number of weeks in the activity are the number of hot water fitters required. The Table 7.11 after the PERT chart gives the normal PERT information, the thick line on the diagram shows the critical path and against each event, is written the earliest (E) and latest (L) event times.

The earliest times (E) are calculated by adding up the activity weeks from the start, down each path. When two or more activities arrive at an event, the highest total of weeks is carried forward to calculate the next earliest times. For example, at event-5, the input path totals are : From event-3, it is seven weeks; from event-1, it is five weeks and from event-4, it is one week, hence seven weeks are carried forward. From event-5 to event-9, it is two weeks, but the earliest time at event-9 is not 'seven weeks plus two weeks equals nine weeks', but 11 weeks. This is because activity-8 to activity-9 is an also input, hence the earliest time carried forward is 11 weeks.

The critical path "is that path with highest totals of earliest times carried forward". To calculate the latest times, we must start at the end of the task, that is event-ten in this instance and work backwards, subtracting all the activity times. Having obtained the earliest and latest times, it is then fairly simple to fill in the table (Refer to Fig. 7.12). Float times are those number of weeks that an activity can "float" between an early start and a late finish, without affecting the total time of the project. This is set by the critical path, where no float exists.

The "total float" is calculated by subtracting the activity time, from the difference between the earliest start and latest finish of the activity. The "free float" is calculated, by subtracting the difference between the earliest and latest finish times from the

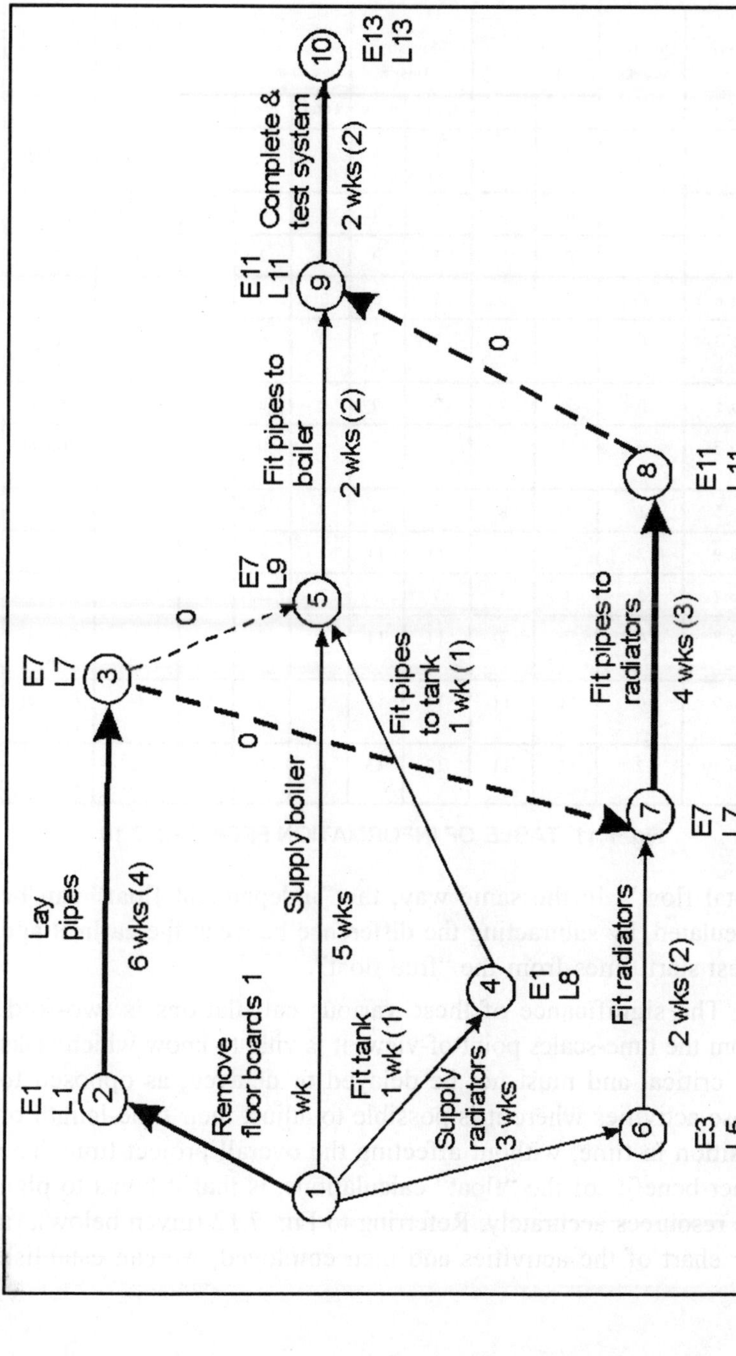

Fig. 7.10. PERT CHART FOR RESOURCE CALCULATION

Activity	Duration Weeks	Start Time		Finish Time		Float			No. of Fitters per week	Remarks
		Early	Late	Early	Late	Total	Free	Ind.		
1 to 2	1	0	0	1	1	0	0	0	—	Critical path
1 to 4	1	0	0	1	8	7	0	0	1	
1 to 5	5	0	0	7	9	4	2	2	1	
1 to 6	3	0	0	3	5	2	0	0	—	
2 to 3	6	1	1	7	7	0	0	0	4	Critical path
3 to 5	0	7	7	7	9	2	0	0	—	Dummy
3 to 7	0	7	7	7	7	0	0	0	—	Critical path
4 to 5	1	1	8	7	9	7	5	−2	1	
5 to 9	2	7	9	11	11	2	2	0	2	
6 to 7	2	3	5	7	7	2	2	0	2	
7 to 8	4	7	7	11	11	0	0	0	3	Critical path
8 to 9	0	11	11	11	11	0	0	0	—	Critical path
9 to 19	2	11	11	13	13	0	0	0	2	Critical path

Fig. 7.11. TABLE OF INFORMATION FROM FIG. 7.10

"total float". In the same way, the "independent float" can be calculated, by subtracting the difference between the earliest and latest start times from the "free float".

The significance of these various calculations is two-fold. From the time-scales point-of-view, it is vital to know which tasks are critical and must not be delayed or delayed, as opposed to those activities where it is possible to adjust their time-length or position in time, without affecting the overall project time. The other benefit of the "float" calculations, is that it helps to plan the resources accurately. Referring to Fig. 7.12 (given below), a bar chart of the activities and men employed, we can establish the weekly demands and histogram of the number of fitters required.

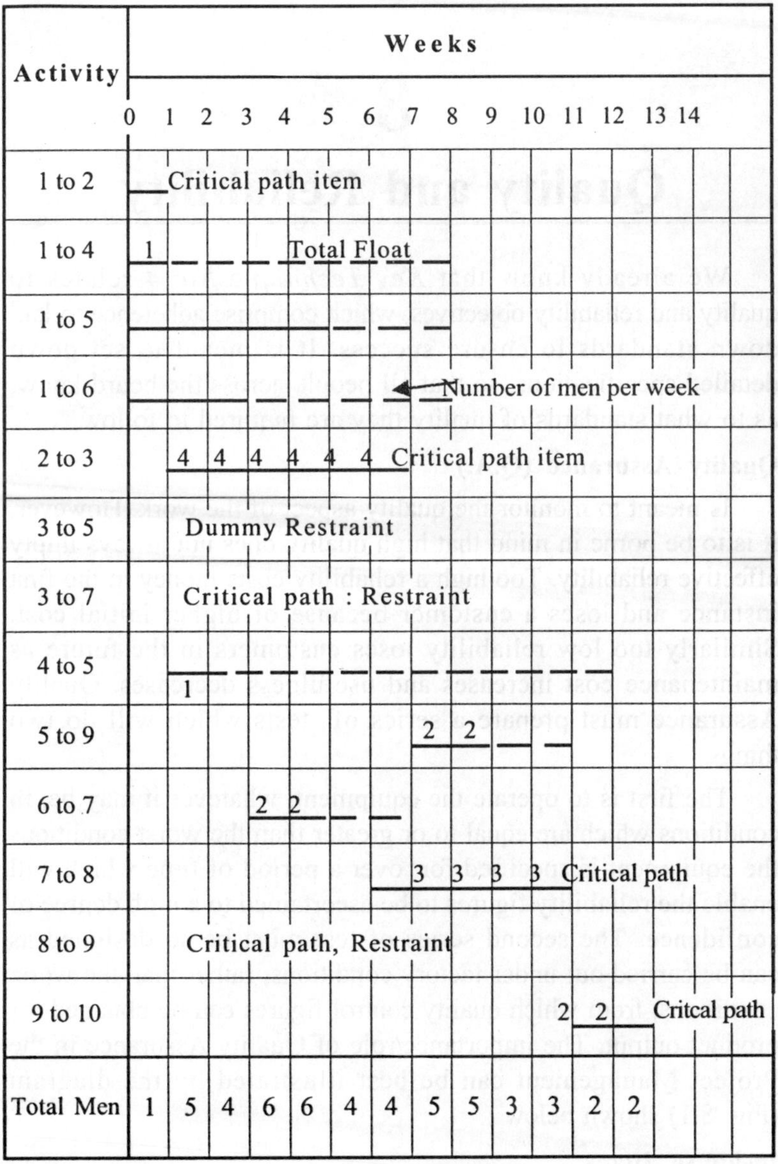

Fig. 7.12. BAR CHART & MANPOWER HISTOGRAM

8

Quality and Reliability

We already know that *Key Technique No. 4* relates to quality and reliability objectives, which comprise adherence to laid down standards to ensure success. It is meant to set down detailed specifications, so that all people across the board know, as to what standards of quality they are required to follow.

Quality Assurance (Q.A.)

Is meant to monitor the quality aspect of the work. However, it is to be borne in mind that high quality does not always imply effective reliability. Too high a reliability costs money in the first instance and loses a customer because of higher initial cost. Similarly too low reliability loses customers in the future as maintenance cost increases and usefulness decreases. Quality Assurance must prepare a series of tests which will do two things.

The first is to operate the equipment, whatever it may be, in conditions which are equal to or greater than the worst conditions the equipment is specified for, over a period of time which will enable the reliability figures to be ascertained to a high degree of confidence. The second series of test must be so designed as can be carried out under factory conditions, rather than the worst conditions, from which quality control figures can be obtained for product output. The importance/role of Quality Assurance in the Project Management can be best illustrated by the diagram (Fig. 8.1) shown below :

In-house Items

This can mean either a standard product line item that the

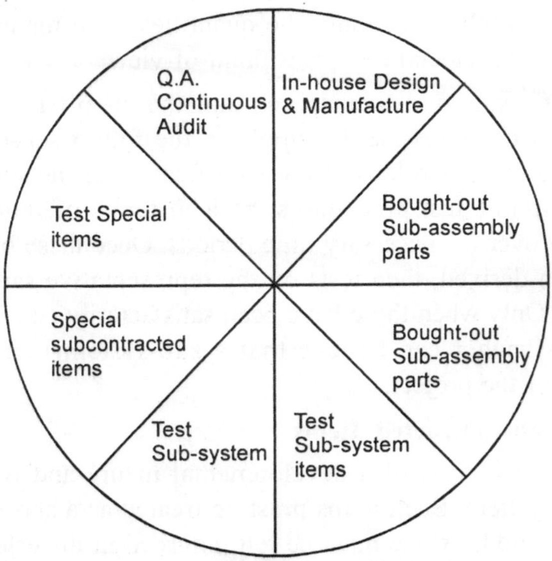

Fig. 8.1. QUALITY ASSURANCE WORK BREAKDOWN

company manufactures or it could be a special item for this project. The Project Manager will be more concerned about Quality Assurance of a special item peculiar to the project. In such cases, he can furnish relevant information in terms of the function and the working environment of the item, to help Quality Assurance carry out proper quality check.

Bought-out Sub-assembly Items

These can cover a very wide range of simple components to fairly complex sub-assemblies. It is likely that the company will already possess Quality Assurance procedures for component level items because of its long standing in the manufacture of such products. In the case of the more complex parts, Quality Assurance shall have to investigate more thoroughly and plan inspection and test procedures, in order that stringent standards of quality and reliability are met.

Bought-out Sub-system Items

The Quality Assurance group have to investigate the standing of the manufacturer who is assigned to supply the complete system, his ability to supply the quantities from manufacturing capacity and financial resources point-of-view.

Having satisfied themselves that the supplier is capable, technically or otherwise, to supply in the fullest sense, Quality Assurance must also look at the specification of the sub-system, evolve suitable test procedures, both in terms of function and reliability over the necessary time periods. Once these procedures have been derived, then tests on the representative samples can be made. Only when these have been satisfactorily concluded, the Project Manager can believe that a sub-system item, will be suitable for the project.

Special Sub-contracted Items

Such an item is of a developmental nature and is, hence a Proprietary Item. Such items must be treated as a sub-project of their own and no stone must be left unturned in the effort, to see that these are as successful and budget conscious as the main project. Quality Assurance must be asked to state the procedures, to inspect and test these items, as well as they do their own in-house items.

The Project Manager must involve the Quality Assurance group in a continuous audit. It can prevent much wastage of time at the end of the project, putting right what really amounts to silly mistakes in terms of quality and reliability by the design engineers who, in this sophisticated and complex technical world must not regard themselves as experts in all things. There can often be disputes, between the design engineers and production engineers. The former want to get on with the design, often in adherence to a tight time-table, sometimes almost regardless of cost; and the latter wants to have the design suitable for the production processes made available. In the circumstances, a Quality Assurance audit can prevent long test and redesign phases by checking. There will be arguments that this is a repetition of the design work, but in actuality this is not so. It is an audit and not a mere repetition of the original work. Quality Assurance audit is an impartial accurate examination of the complete design picture.

In the coordination of any job, where all or some of the items (as given in Fig. 8.1) apply, the Project Manager must use the services of Quality Assurance as much as possible, as it can considerably help him in achieving a trouble free and smooth running project.

Quality Control

Is the important function of carrying out tests, inspections and analyses to ensure, that quality throughput is as laid down in the Quality Assurance standards. It is most beneficial to the manufacturing and design processes. It involves inspection throughout every part of the product line to ascertain that the Quality Assurance (Q.A.) and Quality Control (Q.C.) departments have agreed as necessary : on the patrol inspection and/or at the end points of the production line (that is the key assembly points) and in the tests of parts or assemblies wholly or partially completed, as well as the whole unit if practicable; and as required by the Quality Control plan.

The Project Manager will of necessity concern himself more with major tests. In many ways the Project Manager is the customer's representative, all through the project task as far as customer is concerned.

9

Product Cost

All though the project, one of the most important tasks for the Project Manager, is to know the product cost. A well designed product is worthless, if nobody will buy it, because it may cost too much or perhaps worse, if the company has contracted to supply at a given cost and finds a substantial loss has been incurred.

In "product cost", we are referring to an end product, which is one of the qualitatively similar kind of items. In this context, the product and project are not synonymous. The project in this case is the activity comprising design, development and manufacture, which enables a quantity of products to be manufactured.

In other cases, the project will be the product, for example a road, a bridge, a dam, an airfield complex, etcetera. In costing a project, which is also a product, we primarily use the budgeting and cost controls. However there are still many items within this chapter that will be useful in the "project equals product" case.

The subject of cost is exceedingly complex, although on the surface it looks deceptively simple. The two main problems here, are multi-project costing and absorption of overheads. In a company making many products, it is almost certain that unless the company is purely project orientated with unshared project facilities, the costs will be spread over all products by standard overhead costing methods. This may be fair in respect of some of the items, for example bought-out materials, but it can be extremely unfair to a successful project, which has to suffer overhead rates from less successful projects. Against this of course, the increases in rates which may arise, even if less successful projects are removed may considerably alter the apparent benefits of cutting them out. In a large company with a large spread of products, the effect of a few unsuccessful products as affecting the costs of the more successful may be quite negligible. The Project Manager is not likely to be able to alter this state of affairs very easily and must, concentrate on his own project with whatever costing methods and rates the company is employing.

As can be seen from the left hand diagram in Fig. 9.1 given below, the final tolerance even with 60 per cent of the items not very well known can be much less. In this example, it is ± 19 per cent unknown of the total. As the costing improves with more knowledge of the product, overall tolerance becomes much more acceptable.

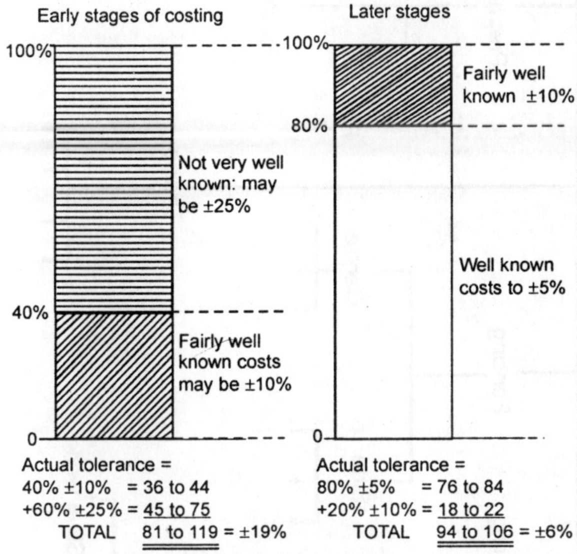

The cost 'pot'

Fig. 9.1. EARLY STAGES OF COSTING

In the search of more and more accurate costing the specification tree, becomes increasingly important.

In case of a new stretch of road, it might be appropriate to start the cost breakdown by major items, as shown in Fig. 9.2. The estimating department will want much assistance from

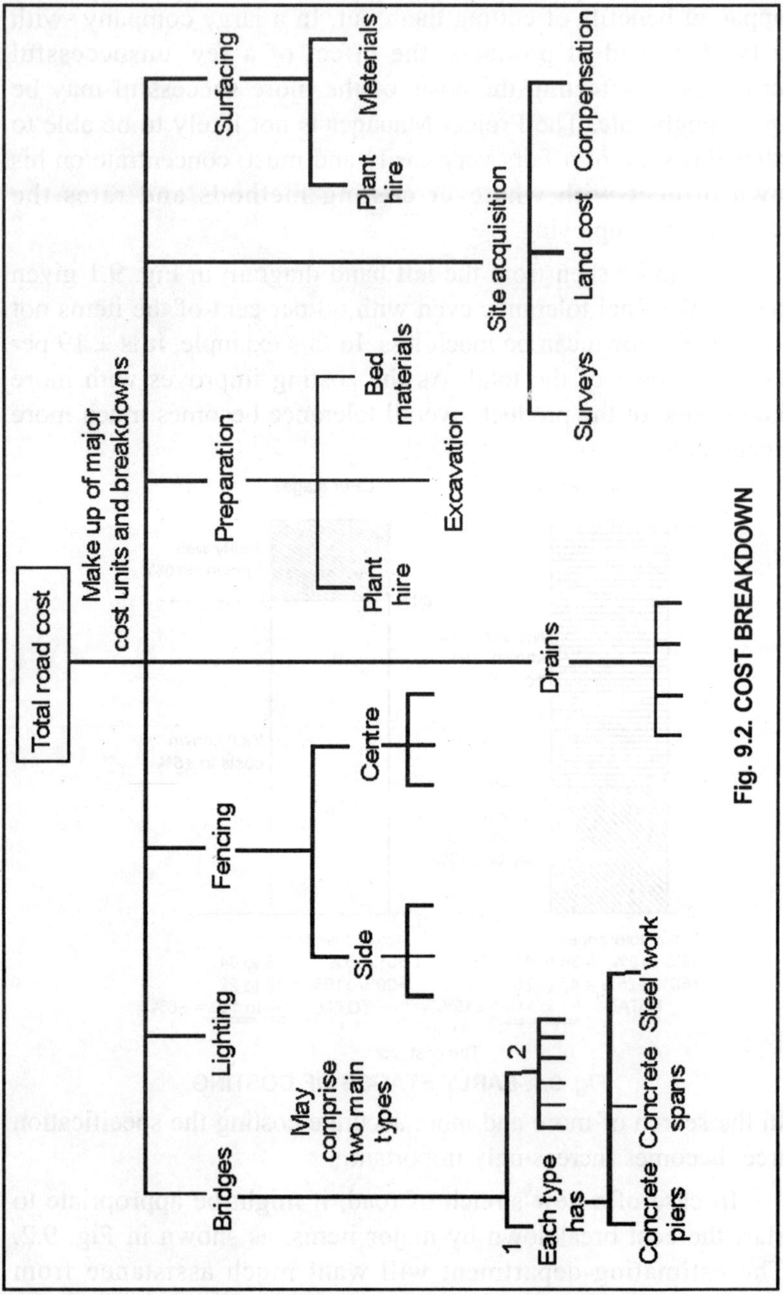

Fig. 9.2. COST BREAKDOWN

designers and others in the early stages of costing as many of the items costed are, but ideas. A practical approach is to compare if possible the likely result of the idea with some item that has gone before. Is it half the size? Is it complex? What does it do compared with this or that product ? Referring to the illustration in Fig. 9.1, it is easier to fix a cost and keep modifying it afterwards. The worst mistake of all is to delay the collation of an initial cost. As the costing progresses with more inputs from drawings, quotations and other information, the inaccuracies will diminish.

Eventually the process sheets will emerge thoroughly costed for some or all of the parts of the processes. At the process sheet stage especially the Project Manager is going to be asked what quantity of the product is going to be sold. This is also an updating necessity as quantity will affect the process in any task. Even in a "one off" job like a road construction the number of miles and number of bridges will affect the plant requirements and methods of doing the job. With any product likely to be manufactured in large quantities, the effect on economies can be very significant with the appropriate choice of process.

A further consideration for the Project Manager is that costing is an ideal subject for computer assistance. A data bank of continually checked and revised unit costs is very necessary for a multi-project company and enables quick and accurate costing to be established.

The Project Manager should be in the best position to aid estimators in choosing a minimum risk and lowest unit cost course — coupled with line management acceptance of the processes and the tooling costs. A further advantage towards rapid cost feedback is in making the use of computer-aided design tools. How can an economic design be produced with inadequate knowledge of costs?

Cost Breakdown

In taking the decision about what estimated cost to present to the management at this stage, when the total tolerances seem large ; it is essential to adopt a standard approach. Whether the answer is intrinsically correct or not, atleast the knowledge of how it was obtained is secure and that other costs will follow the same pattern can be taken for granted. By feedback from actual results, it will be possible to correct the arithmetic's in the process. Referring to the statistical illustration given below, at an early stage we can have a product cost breakdown as given in Table 9.3 :

TABLE 9.3

Early Stage Product Cost Breakdown

Unit No.	Cost Breakdown Rs. (lakhs)
Unit-1	1±25%
Unit-2	2±5%
Unit-3	10±10%
Unit-4	30±15%
Unit-5	40±10%
Unit-6	60±20%
Unit-7	100±5%
Unit-8	1±50%
Unit-9	50±5%
Unit-10	20±20%

Tolerances

What is total cost that should be passed upto the top management? There is a low probability that all tolerances will be high or low together, so some statistical correction is legitimate. A simple method often used and capable of repetition and checking at a later stage, is to take "the square root of the mean of the sum of the squares of the tolerances (the root mean square of the tolerances) as follows :

In the above table 9.4, the mean of squares is 22,882/10, that is 2286; and *v ? (Tolerance)²/n = v2286 = 47*. Maximum Tolerance of cost = Rs. 3135 lacs ± 338. Statistical correction gives Rs. 3135 lacs ± 47.

TABLE 9.4

A Simple Example of Total Cost

Unit	Cost (Rs. in lakhs)	Total (In %)	Tolerance	(Tolerance)^2
1	1	25	2.5	6.25
2	1.5	5	0.75	0.5625
3	10	10	10	100
4	30	15	45	2025
5	40	10	40	1600
6	60	20	120	14,400.00
7	100	5	50	2,500.00
8	1	50	5	25
9	50	5	25	625
10	20	20	40	1600
Total	313.5		± 338.25 Maximum Tolerance	22,881.81

If one figure only has to be given, then bearing in mind the well known law that " if things can go wrong they will", it would probably be wise to estimate Rs. 3182.0 lacs for the complete production of 10 units. All the above relies on the fact that the original costing have been absolutely honest, that is there really is just as much chance of the estimated cost being more or less within the tolerance stated. If the tolerance is estimated to be unequal, for example between five per cent to 20 per cent, then the statistics will demand more arithmetic!

Cost Accounting

The Project Manager will find it highly desirable to know as much as possible about the cost accounting in his company. Even in the best accounting systems, there can still be arguments as to how the product should be costed. He must strive to fight for his project cost to reflect the real cost, no matter if it is good or bad news.

10

Meetings, Communication and Presentation of Information

In Project Management there will be a maximum of communication because this is an important facet of Project Management towards the project's success. To know the problem is a good portion of the battle won and people know it is only achieved by maximum communication. Meetings will be necessary because humans are bad at interpretation. We all need unambiguous definitions. A lot of these will have to be cleared up at meetings.

Meetings

There are key techniques for meetings as well as Project Management itself. Firstly, there must be an object. Secondly, the right people must be there because it serves no good having a meeting, if the people sent cannot decide anything. Thirdly, the meeting must be competent enough to decide upon the subject, which must stay within the scope of the meeting level and ability. Fourthly, sufficient notice with the objectives clearly stated on an agenda must be sent to the right people, after ensuring that they can be present.

There are four ways in which a meeting can proceed, *viz.*

The free-for-all meeting which has no definite results; the Chairman's recital which turns out to be a monologue and not a meeting; a conglomeration of silent men where no one dares to speak; or it can be an effective logical, responsive decision making process!

If you want a meeting. Have a meeting. But don't use it as an excuse to give a lecture to a captive audience. You will have an agenda, because the objectives have already been stated. As far as possible, stick to the agenda. There is always the chance that an important additional item may arise out of the meeting. Be prepared to deal with it. Do not make silent men, by admonishing them, if they are slightly irrelevant. Guide them gently back to the target agenda, instead of driving them to silence. See to it that there is no free-for-all dialogue. Common courtesies to each other and to the Chairman, must be the order of the day.

The Agenda of the Meeting

Meetings have to be without long and fruitless dialogues. It is helpful to adopt some standard pattern so that the facts are stated, without having to think too much about them. A clear agenda will help to get the business done by keeping people to the point.

Minutes of the Meeting

These should be action notes, not an essay to describe how a number of people spent an afternoon. There are ofcourse, exceptions to every rule. Like if the meeting took place to prepare a report on some subject for example, saying for higher management, then a more detailed report is expected rather than action notes. The majority of meetings however, are more effective in deciding what actions shall take place by agreement, and within the competence and authority of the meeting.

Communication

In a larger company, people have to communicate a great deal. The type of communication to keep people informed, especially within the Project Management organization is important, because there will be constant dangers of cutting across company lines of communication. If this occurs accompanied with lack of communication, friction could result. There may also be a mixture of annoyance, fright and frustration.

Information

In many cases, written words, lists or tabulations may carry the same information, but the clarity and speed of information transfer can often be much more effective by graphical presentations, for example, charts.

Charts

Charts are of varying categories and appearances. But, these can generally be said to be based upon a few basic types, *viz.* :

Graph or Curve is the commonest of all charts.

Surface Chart is a graph with a continuous line joining the coordinate points, but this time the surface under the line is hatched with line or cross pattern which gives an impression of the size or magnitude as well as the movement associated with a graph. (Refer to Fig. 10.1)

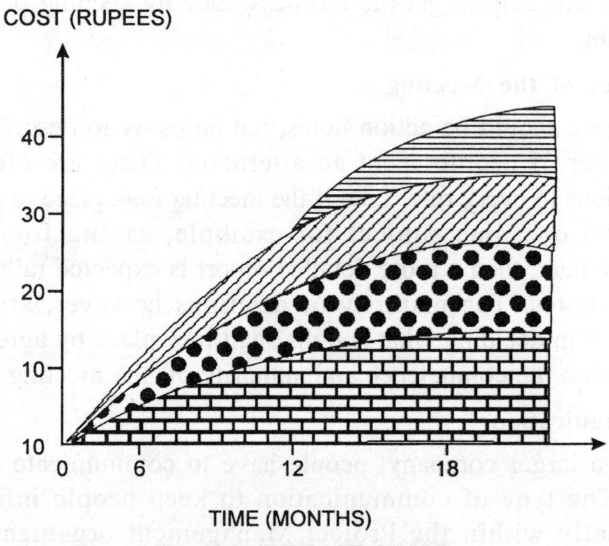

Fig. 10.1. SURFACE CHART

Bar Chart has several versions, the most common of which involves comparison bars against targets. (Shown in Fig. 10.2)

Pie or Circle Chart is the familiar "how much slice of cake" diagram.

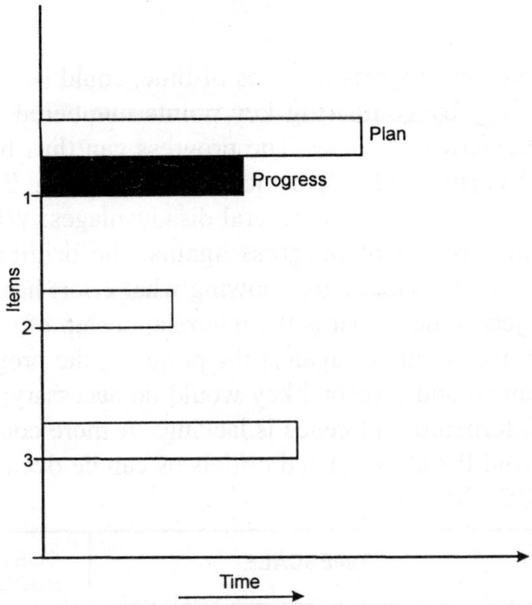

Fig. 10.2. BAR CHART

Column Chart has vertical bars that are used to represent a value of one sort or another, but not necessarily on any time-scale.

Management Information

Presentation of information to management and staff at all levels requires much thought, patience and observation by the Project Manager. Presentation has to be adjusted to the level of management or staff receiving it. The presentation to the higher management must be self-explanatory. It is unlikely that the first report will completely succeed in its purpose, but it is essential to find a solution compatible with the needs of higher management.

Under this facet, the key areas for management will revolve around the following : Setting costs against budgets at the time; the progress against plans at the time; forecasts of costs to be incurred, as well as projections of the progress completions; and the problem areas. These must be clearly presented, with the interrelating factors adequately highlighted.

Time

The project progress in terms of time, could be illustrated in a simple way by comparing key points numbered 1, 2, 3 etc. against the actual progress. The progress can thus be shown in two lines earmarked : "planned" and "actual". But such an illustration can suffer from several disadvantages: When there is no current forecast of progress against the original plan; no provision has been made for showing what effort has been made in the project to date, that is the interrelationship of cost in terms of money and resources against the progress; the progress points are not named and a special key would be necessary; as also the back up information reference is lacking. A more comprehensive way to avoid the above stated criticisms can be deciphered from the Fig.10.3 given below.

TIMESCALE							COST vs BUDGET	
Ref	Item	M	Pert Date	M	Actual Achievement	Current Forecast	Budget (Rs)	Actual
1	Project Start	J	1.1.94				1.0	
		F		F	10.2.94			
		M	15.3.94	M			2.5	3.5
2	First Proto-type built	A						
		M		M	15.5.94			
3	First Proto-type testing	J	1.6.94	J			5.0	7.5
		J			1.7.94			
		A		A			Review	1.8.94
4	Engin-eering Drawing comple-ted	S	1.9.94	J				
		O		O				
		N		A		1.11.94		

Fig. 10.3. COST/TIME SUMMARY SHEET

Costs

An indicative graph of costs versus budget, together with progress on the task is shown in the Fig. 10.4. This graphic is quite comprehensive and ideal, in many ways for a quick management appraisal. It is likely to be acceptable only when it is supported by all back-up information, that is available at all

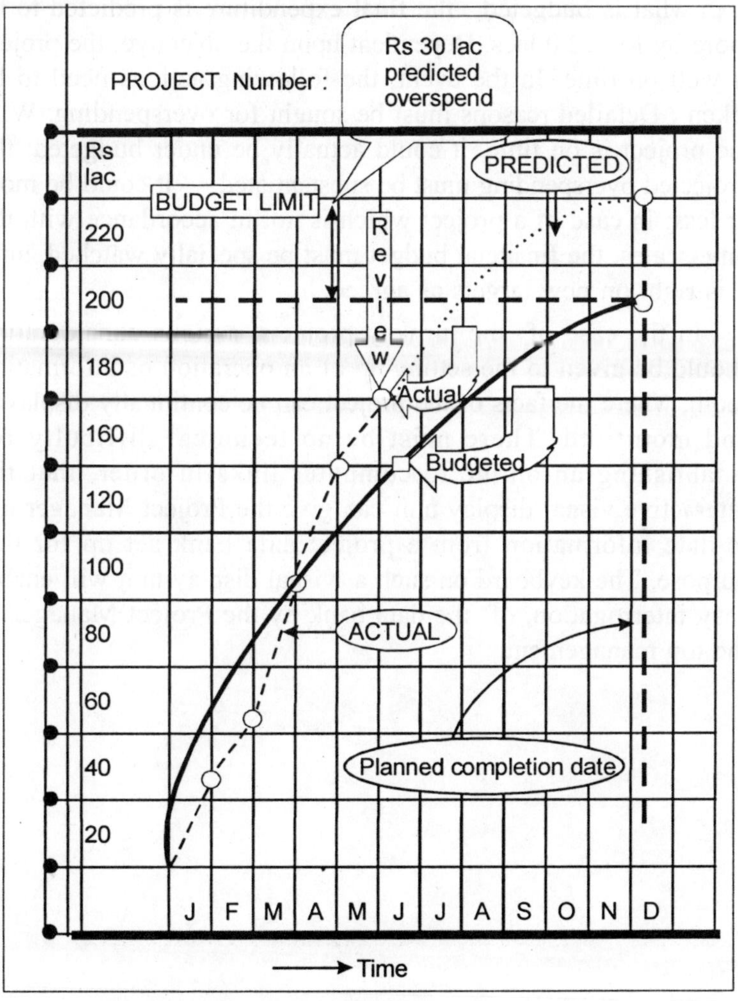

Fig. 10.4. PROGRESS COST CONTROL SHEET

times, to measure the project's progress accurately enough. But it is not always easy to assess accurately the successful completion, of these milestones and some risk may inevitably have to be taken.

The following conclusions can be drawn from the study of the cost control sheet given in Fig. 10.4, *viz.* : Expenditure is more than what is budgeted; the final expenditure is predicted to be more by Rs. 12.0 lacs. Dependent upon the objective, the project is well on time. In the event, the following actions need to be taken : Detailed reasons must be sought for overspending. With the project is on time, it could actually be under budgeted; the projected overspending must be substantiated — it could be more or less; in case of a project which is not in accordance with the time-scales, the financial budget must be specially watched, until it is right on new targets as agreed.

In the case of the turnkey projects, serious consideration should be given to the setting up of an operation or information room, where the facts of the project can be continually displayed and monitired. There must be no technical difficulty for establishing an online to computer links in order, that the interactive visual display unit can give the Project Manager up-to-date information from a project data bank set up for this purpose. The keyboard on such a visual display unit will enable easy interrogation, of the data bank by the Project Manager or the top management.

11
Project Control

The whole concept of Project Management is to know, interpret and control the whole project as distinct from any one functional management part, for example design, manufacture or testing. The project is viewed continuously as one integrated whole task. This puts a greater responsibility on the Project Manager to report accurately, efficiently, rapidly and clearly upon the project progress. There must be, no secrets from top management; no lack of planning because warnings of trouble come too late; dissemination of information must be adjusted as necessary to all levels of management and staff; and the progress information must be provided in a form acceptable to the recipient.

Equally there must be no exemption for the top management : In not providing management backing for the project and the Project Manager; as well as, in not trying to appreciate new ways of information presentation, for example PERT, display terminals, etc. The management information charts are the balance sheets of situations after careful investigations. This sort of searching for truth in itself provides a control.

Referring back to the project identification triangle, Fig. 6.1, we showed four levels as an example. Control consists of checking a series of key events in each level of the identification hierarchy. Each top level key event is completely specified as a major objective on baseline, so that no lack of clarity or ambiguity can obscure a positive achievement. To proceed past one of these objectives without it being achieved in all respects may be a decision of the highest management or the Company's Board of Directors. On the other hand, the Project Manager may be authorized to make all decisions from the start with the aid of the company's specialist organization.

Below these top level objectives come the second level and other levels which will normally be within the scope of the Project Manager's authority. All events have to be specified in terms of technical progress and cost as originally conceived. These keys events may have hundreds of activities between them and the number of levels of the reporting system is chosen accordingly. The whole concept is to set objectives at varying levels, of the task and manage the project, by assessing the achievement of these objectives. The lower level objectives are just as much the real links in the chain, and are all too often ignored.

Identification of Objectives

We have already stated that the objectives must be fully specified, so that we are clearly aware whether we have met them. There is no doubt identifying objectives, is a critical area of control. Each of the objectives in a project work entails two main areas of management as regards, *viz.* :

Financial

We cannot accept on its own merit a statement of underspending, being on target or overspending.

Underspending

This may not be serious, as the budget may have been too high. How exactly are we to judge this criteria? Is it against progress ? Is the project behind the schedule? Have the resources been deployed correctly?

Overspending

Similar remarks (as stated for underspending) apply. The overspending may or may not be serious. It has to be weighed against the progress and the original budget. Even being on course with spending can have any of the pitfalls of overspending or underspending.

Summarily, the above stated facets cannot be isolated. They must be weighed against each other and any additional control information that can be brought to bear. Progress can be even more difficult to assess because unlike money, it cannot always be counted in units. If one of our objectives in the lower level of key events hierarchy is measured against its specification on due date and fails for some reason, is the whole programme to be stopped while we wait for the objective to be fully achieved? Probably not, but we might take risk immediately if we proceed. A decision has to be made : Will this deficiency slow up the project now or later? Rules and specifications like budgets can be ignored at times but we must know, record and watch with even more attention, the subsequent progress to see if our decision was right.

Costs Analysis and Control

In the make up of project costs, derived from the addition of all the packages of work or sub-jobs that make up the total, the costs will vary according to the resources put in to them. This sounds very simple and obvious, but there is a third effect — "time".

If a task costs Rs. 1,000 per week with two men involved and normal time is of ten week's duration, the cost is clearly Rs. 10,000. If we now want to cut the down time to eight weeks, it is certain that the cost will go up beyond the estimated Rs. 10,000. This is so, due to the extra men employed and overtime costs as well as the charges for mechanical aids deployed, if any. In addition, there may be a minimum time for the task, no matter what extra money is spent. Conversely, if the time exceeds the scheduled ten weeks, the cost may not fall below the additional cost of Rs. 1,000 per week. These two simple truisms of project costs, produce the project cost curve as illustrated in Fig. 11.1.

While the graphical presentation in Fig.11.1 appears to be simple, it is usually not so easy to put figures on the graph and draw the correct curve for a particular project. If, however, we

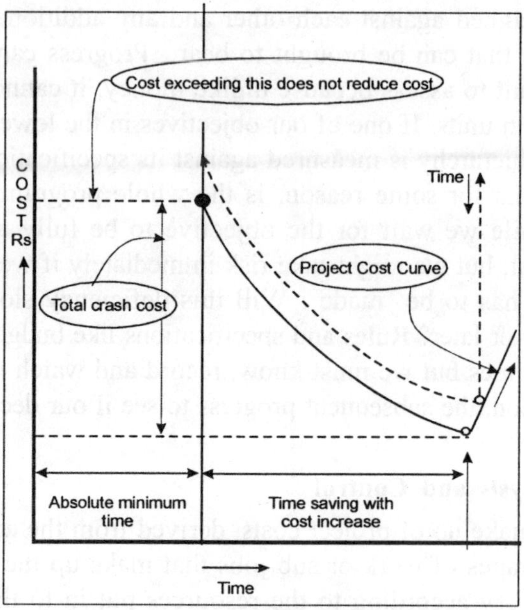

Fig. 11.1. PROJECT COST CURVE

are to control the costs properly, we must try and find out as much as possible about them and their relationship to the time-scale. This information is essential for the following reasons :

In the initial timing and costing of the project, we need to know what time-scale we can achieve for Rs. (x) costs, even when it may not be possible to achieve it at all for Rs. (x)!;

Given a certain time-scale, what will the cost be? If the project is running late, how much will it cost to bring it back on time, if needed, if at all it can be done. If the project time-scale has to be shortened, even though the project is on time, the crash cost/time relationship must be known. The costs of all activities on the project network must be known to satisfy the first two requirements of the four cited above, including additional costs, both "crash" and "late" costs. In respect to lateness and crash action, we need to know more about the critical and the near-critical path items. This can be done with computer assistance to

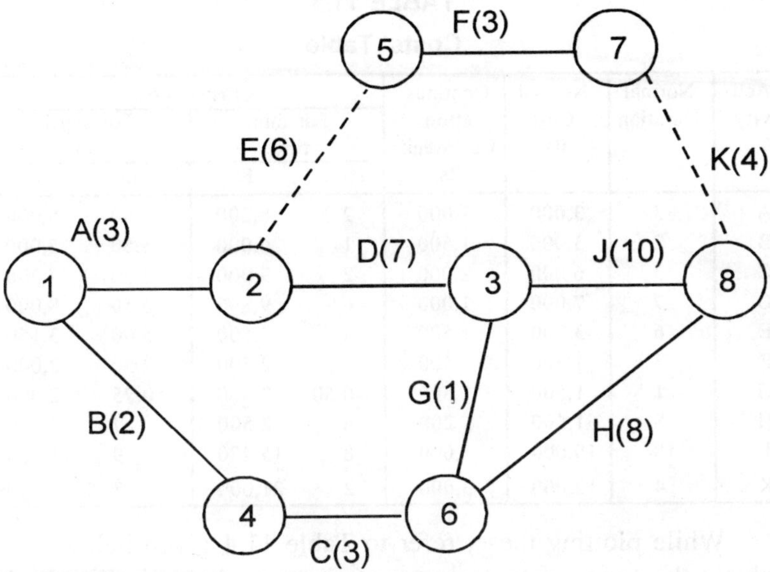

Fig. 11.2. PERT DIAGRAM FOR COST CURVE

perform full cost and resource analysis. The two are obviously closely interlinked.

Construction of a Project Cost Curve

To do this we need to know the "normal" costs, the "continuation" costs and the "crash" costs on the network critical and the near critical paths.

In Fig. 11.2 (given above) is a PERT (Programme Evaluation and Review Technique) network at normal times (in weeks), prepared in order to establish the base for the next steps.

The table (please refer to Table 11.3) sets down the estimated "normal" costs and the cost of reducing the time-scale. These costs have to be found by obtaining alternative estimates for different cost approaches for each activity. Examining now only the critical path of activities A, D and J (as given in Fig. 11.2) have the following cost characteristics as shown in Fig. 11.3.

TABLE 11.3
Costs' Table

Activity	Normal Duration	Normal Cost Rs.	Continuation Cost/week Rs.	Crash Costs: For min. time — Time	Crash Costs: For min. time — Rs.	Crash Costs: For stated time — Time	Crash Costs: For stated time — Rs.
A	3	3,000	1,000	2	8,200	2.50	5,000
B	2	3,000	1,500	1	6,000	1.50	5,000
C	3	6,000	2,000	2	9,000	2.50	7,300
D	7	7,000	1,000	6	9,800	6.50	8,000
E	6	3,000	500	4	2,500	5.00	3,150
F	3	1,500	500	2	2,500	2.50	2,000
G	1	1,500	1,500	0.50	2,500	0.75	2,000
H	8	1,600	200	6	2,500	7	2,000
J	10	10,000	1,000	8	15,400	9	11,300
K	4	12,000	3,000	2	21,000	3	16,000

While plotting these, refer to Table 11.4 given below. We obtain the appropriate project cost curve as shown in Fig. 11.4. It is to be noticed that the limits on critical path items did not cause an encroachment into the next critical path, that is event-eight, which if we suffered the extra crash costs, is now at week-16 instead of week-20. This is equal to E-F-K. If the reduction in time on the critical path could have brought event-eight below 16 weeks, then activities E, F and K would have to be examined to see if these could be reduced.

A further point to be taken note of at the time reduction on critical path is, where the significant differences exist in the

Crash Cost/Time

Activity	Stated: Time saved (In weeks)	Stated: Cost (In Rs.)	Minimum: Time saved (In weeks)	Minimum: Cost (In Rs.)	Construction Costs (In Rs./ per week)
A	0.5	2000	1	5200	1000
D	0.5	1000	1	2800	1000
J	1	1300	2	5400	1000

Fig. 11.4. CONSTRUCTION OF PROJECT COST CURVE

TABLE 11.5

An Example Showing Crash Costs

Planned Completion	Project Cost (Rs. in Lakhs)	Cumulative Penalties (Rs. in Lakhs)	Crash Costs (extra expense in Rs.)	Total (Rs. in Lakhs)
Budget	2.33	Nil	0.8	3.13
1 week late	2.43	0.05	0.45	2.93
2 week late	2.53	0.1	0.08	2.71
3 week late	2.63	0.15	0.03	2.81
4 week late	2.73	0.2	Nil	2.93

increases in costs per week saved, the lower cost items should be adjusted first to decrease the slope of the crash cost curve, that is, make c/t — a minimum.

Penalties and Crash Costs

If the project is running late and penalties are likely, then some simple arithmetic with project cost curve and penalty build-up will enable the most economic solution to be found. We will assume the project is running four weeks late and the penalties are Rs. 50,000 per week for late delivery; crash costs have the form according to Fig. 11.4. The crash cost and the budget will be spent at the original planned date. From Table 11.5 (Crash Costs), it can be seen that an acceptance of two weeks' penalty would be the cheapest solution rather than incurring any more crash costs.

Making Decisions, Especially Technical ones

The science of decision making is obviously going to be affected very much by a particular industry and its needs. It is almost certain that the Project Manager cannot be an expert in all skills involved, though he will however, know the language. There will be other managers or staff with specialist skills. We must reply on the man we chose in the particular skill area to make decisions on problems, involving that skill unless and until, we assess that he is not capable enough. It may then be decided by the Project Manager to seek other specialists' opinions. There is nothing wrong in this. It is not a question of mistrust of the man initially consulted.

Generally, it is essential to have more than one solution for the problem. Judgment can then be applied. *Key Techniques 1, 2* and *3* are still the base of the decision making process. Once the decision is made we can move on.

The Project Manager, above all things, must not believe that he is an expert in all the skills. For the production engineering problem, he should get the best production engineers around him and the same applies to all other skills. The further we advance into this technological age, the more complex the projects, the shorter the time-scales; then the ideal combination is Project Management organization and techniques coupled with the best specialist skills.

Changes

The progress of the project will be marked by achievements of objectives. There will also, be a set of manufacturing drawings produced as progress of the project allows. These drawings and accompanying information are committing the company to a way of manufacture and manufactured items. It is vital that the Project Manager exercises firm control with the help of Quality Assurance and project engineers over the following areas :

The production engineering for correct product tooling, use of correct plant and machinery, and use of right processes.

The state of drawings for engineering standards, and correct state of the design.

The change control over drawings for changes due to production engineering, and changes for technical reasons at the design stage or the manufacturing stage or field reports. Changes cost money; wrong drawings cost money; wrong processes cost money; so everything costs money. The real point at issue is that the drawings must be as correct as possible. There will be changes continually produced and we must control the procedure to filter them.

Change Control

Unless changes are firmly controlled, the project will almost certainly be late and more costly. Once a project key objective is passed, there should be the utmost resistance to any change affecting that key objective. However when you get down to the earthy job of running a project, it does not seem so easy to resist change. Class 1 changes are generally considered to be essential and affect baselines. Because of the believed essential nature of these changes, there is all the more reason for a very thorough vetting of them with a cost and time penalty firmly assessed.

Class-1 changes may invariably affect : Specified function; performance; maintainability; reliability; system interfaces and perhaps, other equipment.

Class-2 changes are desirable, but not essential. These could include items such as color of paint, of internal metal work not conforming to drawing, but which could be considered tolerable; of cables which may be too long; etc.

There is an *engineering change control* department which, while the project is at the prototype development stage, receives copies of changes raised by engineers. Once the prototype development has been concluded, the manufacturing drawings have to be issued for Quality Assurance tests and examination. Quality Assurance concludes testing and examination of the prototype and includes vetting of the manufacturing methods. The engineering control department will examine the functional aspects, before product approval is accorded. Thereafter manufacturing drawings for detailed parts are released for production, after which all changes are rigorously examined and have to pay their way.

The whole point of formal change procedure is not to stop necessary changes, but to eliminate unnecessary ones and above all, to provide to the management the knowledge of the cost, advantages and disadvantages of the change actions.

12 Subcontractors

At some stage in every project, it will be necessary to consider putting some work out to subcontract. This may become clear right from the start or it may become clear as the planning of the project proceeds.

The subject of subcontractors is sometimes, an emotive one. At the one extreme are those who grudge the profit made by a subcontractor and who believe that all work, should be done "in house" to secure all the profits available in the project to themselves. At the other extreme are those who want to subcontract out as much as possible to subcontractors, due to the heavy mark-up added to the price for company overheads. Whether or not to employ subcontractors must be decided on the basis of facts in each case. The criterion for judging is basically that of profit.

In selecting the subcontractor, the following guidelines can be helpful :

- Whether the subcontractor has the necessary capability with regards to his specialist's knowledge and skill?
- Whether he has the necessary plant and equipment to carry out the job?
- Whether he is well established with adequate financial strength?

After proper assessment of the above stated factors, tenders should be invited. Weightage should be given to the best price and delivery terms quoted. It has to be ensured that the subcontractor has studied the job fully and appreciates its complexities. To obtain sound tenders, it is necessary to have explained in detail to applicants about what is required. At the same time, the Project Manager should establish what the work is worth and how the price should be built up.

Controlling Subcontractors

Problems regarding control of subcontractors fall into two areas *viz.* : the commercial and the practical.

The problem is to ensure that the contract covers the needs of the situation. The *Commercial Points* that should be covered in the contract are : Price; requirements of contract; delivery; maintenance; quality and acceptance tests; guarantees; insurance and liabilities; and penalties.

(i) *Price :* In considering the "Price" element in the contract, the time value of money must be remembered. In one large project in the automobile industry, the main contractor found that he eventually paid Rs. 50,000 more than he had bargained for on a Rs. 10,00,000 contract. He let the terms in his own contract with the customer get out of line with the subcontract terms. As a result the contract with the subcontractor provided for the progress payments, whereas the main contract did not. The main contractor then had the problem of finding money before he was due to be paid. Fortunately the main contractor was a large company and able to raise the money.

However the cost in interest payments of making progress payments was Rs. 50,000 and that reflected nastily into the profits on the whole contract. Price is a straight forward enough concept. However in overseas projects, the price may be expressed in a foreign currency, in which case there should be provision for the effects of changes in currency exchange rates. It may also be necessary to specify the place of payment and if this is overseas to consider how the payment will be affected by currency transfer regulations. It may be necessary to buy foreign currency forward to meet the contract commitments or it may be desirable to insure against currency risks.

Requirements of the Contract : The requirements covered

by the price must be crystal clear. Does the price cover test equipment and initial stock of spares? Does the price cover the provision of manuals and if so how many copies? If the equipment ordered is to be linked with other equipment, what are the arrangements for technical support during linking and testing? In fact, the project must be thought right through to the end and all requirements to be placed on the subcontractor must be identified and covered in the contract. Even if all items cannot be specified, it must be clear as to what is covered under the price. There must also be an agreement on how extras will be priced.

(ii) *Delivery :* The delivery date must be in accord with the PERT chart for the project and the place of delivery must also be stated. Delivery time should be on the basis of delivery at site. Loading/unloading, transportation and insurance coverage up to installation and commissioning should come in the contractor's scope, if required at extra cost.

(iii) *Maintenance :* Provision must be made for maintenance in the contract. If the subcontractor is to do maintenance, what will be its basis? Will he provide a resident engineer? Or will it be on call basis? Training of company's engineers for satisfactory operation of the equipment should be included in the contract. Supply of spares has to be ensured. Prices of consumable spares and preventive maintenance spares should be quoted, at the time of the signing of the contract.

(iv) *Quality :* The quality of the work done by the subcontractor, is a prime concern of the Project Manager. The success of the whole project depends upon it. The quality of the work must therefore, be specified and carefully checked against the specifications.

(v) *Guarantees :* The smooth running of the project once it "goes live" will depend upon the continued good performance of all component parts of the installation, including those supplied or built by the subcontractors. Keeping this mind, a performance guarantee clause should form part of the contract. There may be some special risks involved in a project arising from technical consideration, which a legal or commercial man may not be able to spot on his own. A Project Manager should highlight these. He must also ensure that any specific requirements, he may have for maintaining control over the subcontractor are included.

(vi) *Penalty :* All projects are time critical. Hence a penalty clause, in the contract is desirable. The penalty clause shall cover both poor performance, as well as delayed deliveries.

In the early stages of a project, all concerned tend to be in an optimistic mood and regard the possibility of actual payment of penalties, as unlikely and discussion of the possibility as academic. But, this possibility is always present. The penalties placed on the subcontractor should line-up with those of the main contractor. A computer manufacturing company tendered for a turnkey project worth about Rs. 1210 lacs. Included in the tender was equipment to be developed by a subcontractor and priced at Rs. 4.50. The final user held out for a penalty clause, giving him a penalty of 0.5 per cent of the price for each week of the delay in the handover date upto maximum of 15 per cent. The subcontractor was only prepared to accept his own "standard" penalty clause, giving 0.25 a week upto a maximum penalty of five per cent.

Finally after a lot of hard negotiating the main penalty was brought down to the maximum of 10 per cent while the subcontractor agreed to accept a penalty of 7.5 per cent. The project was important to the main contractor. It was a key step to establishing himself in a potentially large overseas market. The project went ahead after signing of the contract. At one stage in the life of the project, things started to go wrong and a realistic look was taken at the penalty situation.

Suppose the project was completed on time except for the subcontractor's equipment, which was 20 weeks late. The penalty would be Rs. 1.20 lacs on the main contract of which only Rs. 15,000 could be recovered from the subcontractors. This was because the subcontractor's penalty did not relate to the value of the whole project but only to the price of his contribution.

Furthermore, the "price" in this case was not the final price of Rs. 4.50 lacs. It was the price which the subcontractor had quoted to the main contractor, that is Rs. 3.0 lacs. In other words the penalty was on Rs. 3.0 lacs and not Rs. 4.50 lacs. Although the subcontractor had accepted a maximum penalty of 7.5 per cent, he would have retained a weekly penalty rate of 0.25 per cent which meant that the main contractor could have suffered maximum penalty at 10 per cent, while the subcontractor was restricted to five per cent only, which was two-thirds of the maximum penalty rate incurred by him.

The above case study amply reveals that there are some points worth considering when establishing penalties to subcontractors in a project. For most subcontractors, a regular system of control is needed. This will vary according to circumstances, but it can probably be built up as a variation around the following : The contractor should be required to produce a time table detailing the main milestones (for large or complex contracts, this should be in the form of a PERT network); and regular meetings should be held and the subcontractor should report progress against the PERT chart.

Although it will be concentrated on critical path events and activities, the report should also confirm that other activities due for completion have in fact been completed. If not completed, a new completion date should be given. Where serious deviation from the plan, either due to slip or because of change of requirements has been accepted, then a revised PERT will be required.

In addition to progress meetings, it will be necessary to have regular technical meetings to solve problems which arise during the course of the work. Where the contract is for equipment to be developed or supplied, it may be desirable to have an engineer or inspector deputed to visit the supplier's or subcontractor's works to monitor the progress. In early stages of a project all concerned tend to be in optimistic mood and regard the actual payment of penalties as unlikely and discussion of the possibility remains purely academic. But the possibility is always there.

13

Programme Evaluation and Review Techniques (PERT)

Programme Evaluation and Review Technique (PERT) and Critical Path Method (CPM), the two facets of the Network Planning Technique, have to a large extent, been responsible for putting the discipline of Project Management on a formal footing.

Project design and network analysis is concerned with the development of the project work plan and project duration time estimates and the evaluation of these in the light of the constraints of the project situation. The strategy selected as a result of the techno-economic analysis forms the starting point of the project design development. The strategy is examined in detail and the details are utilized to compile the sequential narration of the constituent activities of the project. This compilation is known as the project logic.

Project logic when represented in the form of a graphical portrayal is called the network. A network generally comprises of a set of symbols connected with each other in a sequential relationship with each step marking the completion of an event. The network diagram and the scheduling computations which follow the development of the network logic, enable the project formulations team to identify the critical path on the longest series of activities through the project construction phase, which determines the project duration. Time-cost trade off and resources leveling techniques are used to, modify these time-estimates and to develop an acceptable work plan for the project.

The most useful results of PERT without doubt is the analytic and critical approach it brings to bear on a project being examined for the first time; the initial review of a project by PERT is probably the most useful attribute. There are millions of people performing tasks great and small and of high or low complexity. Many of these tasks will succeed without PERT. Some may fail even with PERT, but in business and technological world the keynote is always to get the dice loaded in favour of success. This means that every artifice or technique that can be brought to bear economically should be brought to bear. For time planning and resource planning, PERT is an excellent practical device. For cost planning and more elaborate resource planning PERT is even more useful, but probably requires a greater understanding to fully succeed in presenting information in a digestible form.

PERT as a Technique

In project management we stress at all times, the need to plan, to maintain control over the plan, and to modify the plan; if we have to, in controlled manner. A large number of project activities give rise to a considerable physical and mental problem in keeping track of each activity and its progress. The real problem lies in interaction; it is a rare occasion, that the progress of one activity does not affect many others.

Gantt charts or bar charts show job layout by time and progress thereof and are exceedingly useful tools. However these charts cannot show continuing interrelation of these jobs, especially when they change in time-scale and resources, unless only a very few activities are involved. In even small sized projects of, say 100 activities, the interrelationship can be complex. PERT is a tidy tool. An isolated activity cannot exist, since it has to be preceeded and succeeded by others, except the first and last activity.

Let us examine the above inferences from the following example. Table 13.1 gives the list of activities for construction of a garden shed. Fig. 13.2 shows what a bar chart might look like, and Fig. 13.3 the PERT diagram.

Table 13.1

LIST OF ACTIVITIES FOR GARDEN SHED

Item No.	Activity or Item	Activity Time (hours)
01	Clear Site	10
02	Dig topsoil away	5
03	Obtain Hardcore	20
04	Lay hardcore foundation	5
05	Obtain ballast	15
06	Obtain cement	15
07	Mix concrete	8
08	Lay concrete	3
09	Obtain bolts	5
10	Set bolts in concrete	2
11	Obtain timber	26
12	Make sides of shed	3
13	Make back of shed	3
14	Make front of shed	4
15	Make roof of shed	3
16	Make door	3
17	Obtain windows	30
18	Fit windows	3
19	Obtain glass to size	10
20	Obtain putty	5
21	Fit glass into windows	3
22	Obtain timber preservatives	5
23	Paint timber with preservatives	3
24	Fit sides, front & back	6
25	Fit roof	3
26	Fit door	3
27	Decide to build shed	}
28	Decide where to build	}
29	Decide what to build	} 30
30	Prepare construction drawing bill of materials	}

You will easily see the principles and quickly recognize that the discipline of a working flow diagram, for that is really what PERT is. PERT to a great extent helps avoid missing the key link activities in the project task.

No.	Activity	Activity Time (individual)
01	Clear Site	10
02	Dig topsoil away	5
03	Obtain Hardcore	20
04	Lay hardcore	5
05	Cbtain blast	15
06	Obtain cement	15
07	Mix concrete	8
08	Lay concrete	3
09	Obtain bolts	5
10	Set bolts	2
11	Obtain timber	25
12	Make sides	3
13	Make back	3
14	Make front	4
15	Make roof	3
16	Make door	3
17	Obtain window	30
18	Fit windows	3
19	Obtain glass	10
20	Obtain putty	5
21	Fit glass	3
22	Obtain preservatives	5
23	Paint timber	3
24	Fit sides, front, back	6
25	Fit roof	3
26	Fit door	3

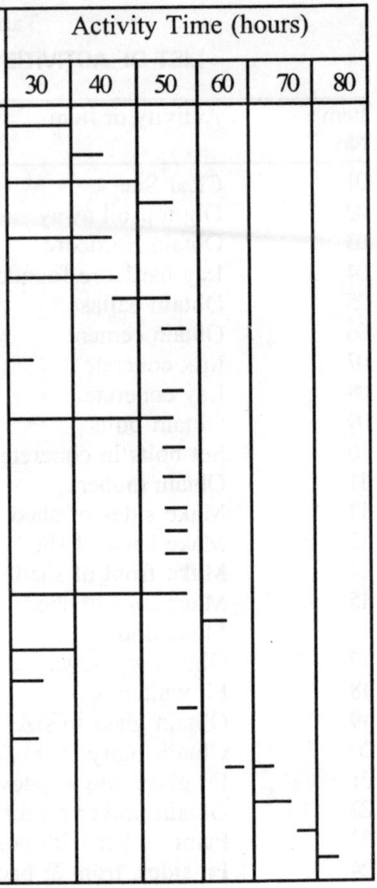

Fig. 13.2. BAR CHART OF ACTIVITIES

Time-Scale

Without questioning the individual times in this example, is the time-scale the shortest that can be achieved? In other words, we can question the logic of the construction. Looking at Fig.13.3, we can see where the critical path runs. Can we rearrange the existing logic to achieve a shorter path? For example, could we put the preservative paint on the shed sections beforehand, rather than right at the end? This would possibly reduce the three hours on the time-scale between activity-13 and activity-14, down to nil

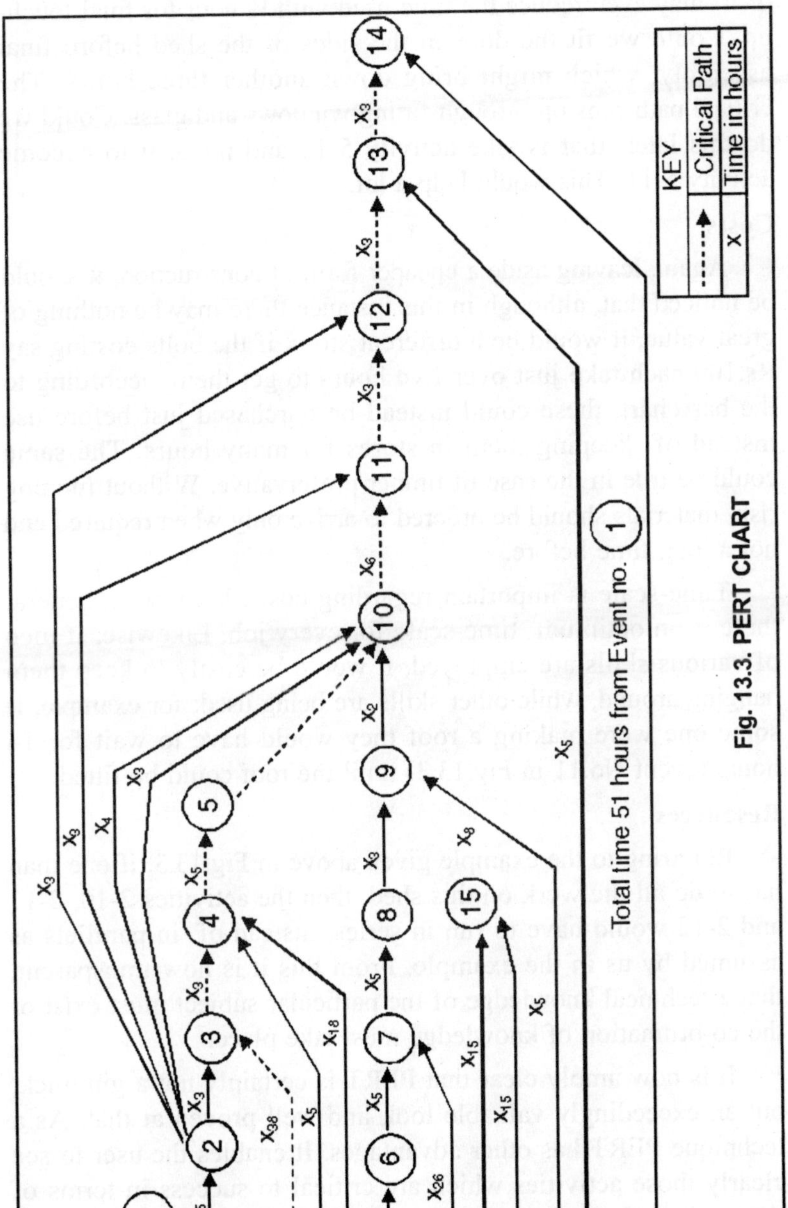

Fig. 13.3. PERT CHART

or it may even reduce the time used with ½ hour for final touch-up. Could we fit the door in the sides of the shed before final assembly, which might bring down another three hours. The critical path runs up through fitting windows and glass. Could we do this later, that is take activity 5-10 and move it to become activity 5-11. This would help a lot.

Costs

Again, leaving aside a cheaper form of construction, it should be noticed that, although in this instance there may be nothing of great value, it would be a different story, if the bolts costing say Rs.100 each take just over five hours to get them, according to the bar chart, these could instead be purchased just before use instead of keeping them in stores for many hours. The same could be true in the case of timber preservative. Without running risk, materials should be ordered to arrive only when required and not a long time before.

Time-scale is important regarding costs, because in general there is an optimum time-scale for every job. Likewise, if men of various skills are employed, it would be costly to keep them hanging around, while other skills are being used; for example, if some one were making a roof they would have to wait for 14 hours (event No.11 in Fig.13.3) until the roof could be fitted.

Resources

Referring to the example given above in Fig.13.3, if one man has to do all the work on this shed, then the activities 2-10, 2-11 and 2-12 would have to run in series, instead of in parallels as assumed by us in the example. From this it is now transparent, that a technical knowledge of the particular subject must exist or the co-ordination of knowledge must take place.

It is now amply clear that PERT is certainly not a gimmick, but an exceedingly valuable tool, and well proven at that. As a technique PERT has other advantages. It enables the user to see clearly those activities which are critical to success in terms of time; those where some delay is acceptable either in the application of lower resources or a delayed start. If delays are experienced on a particular activity, the effects can be seen almost immediately because of the activity linking.

With PERT, many methods of presenting information have been evolved, that is the earliest or latest start dates or finish dates; allowable delays; critical path activities; activities in allowable delay order, etc. These aid the Project Manager to instantly observe the project position. As a technique, it is of great advantage to a lot of firms as well as professionals because it is a logical and intensely useful tool for Project Management.

Developing the Project Logic

Project logic can be defined as the descriptive narration of the constituent activities of a project in a sequential and correlated manner. Project strategy and the techno-economic profile of the project, forms the base for the development of the project logic. Completion of a project presupposes the successful undertaking of a number of activities. These activities may be undertaken concurrently with each other or as of necessity to be taken up one after the other. Project logic analyzes the optimal project strategy that must be synergized into the work elements, which are parallel continuous series of activities having same start and end events.

The work elements can be divided into individual activities. After the identification of the activities, the interrelationship between these activities is determined so as to define the project corelationships. Determination of activity interrelationship is one of the most important aspects in the network development exercise. Whether a particular set of activities should be taken in series or parallel with another set depends on a large number of factors.

Physical and technological dependency and time and resource constraints are the more important factors. Physical and technological dependency define the activity interrelationships in absolute terms. If in physical or technological terms, one activity cannot be undertaken before the other is completed, no choice in the matter is available. The project logic has to accept this constraint as a basic limitation. The corelationship between work elements in a project is however, to a large extent dependent upon the time and resource constraints. It is possible to run several work elements as parallel activities, if the time and resource constraints so permit.

Time and Resource Estimation

After a PERT chart is finally produced showing the logic of the work flow, the logic in terms of detailed activity times has to be weathered. Many genuine difficulties beset individuals, who are assigned the onerous job of estimating time and resources for a project. Some of the problems which may appear are as stated below :

Has the job been specified sufficiently? On an even basis of reasonable specifications, has the management given clear indication of what resources will be available for fruition of the project? Has the type of work that the project demands been accomplished before? If not. Is there sufficient information available to enable sensible estimates to be made? Should other colleagues be consulted? Will their estimates be better ? What if the estimates are wrong. Can these be changed? Should some hidden contingency be added? Will there be trouble, if the estimates prove wrong?

To overcome the difficulties of contributors, the Project Manager must see that the task is understood as thoroughly as is possible at that time. Encouragement must be given to the contributors so they seek out the truth themselves, to identify themselves with the project and assist in defining the tasks. Contributors must search both inside and outside the company for relevant information, from which the best estimates can be prepared. The basic data for activity information must be sought out extremely carefully. Cross checking where necessary is therefore also essential, so that the maximum experience can be obtained to bear on the information.

It obviously does make a difference whether a senior staff or junior staff is assigned to work on the actual job. In general, the contributor at the lower level should not ignore the resource availability as far as possible. He should state that it would take, say 6 weeks to do a particular job and he has allowed certain resources to the job. As the PERT plan moves up the management tree, the awareness of resources and the likelihood what resources will be available will increase, and a balancing process will take place. This will first be done in conjunction with the original contributor who can state his case in detail.

Contributors must have confidence in themselves and their management. The Project Manager must support them in times of stress so that they do not feel inhibited from estimating and correcting estimates, if it necessary to do so. One of the difficult functions of a Project Manager is to assess whether by the changes incorporated in the progress, success can be anticipated and what personnel he can rely on for accurate estimates and assessments.

Contingencies

This subject is both a blessing and a curse. Individual contributors, after assessing a task by whatever process, should not need to add contingencies. They must be prepared to defend in a professional manner their estimates before the management. The management in their wisdom may add contingencies, provided they are at a high enough level of the network. Let the best estimates by the qualified people be subjected to proper management investigation, before adjusting the results if necessary.

Contingency may be added in clear and visible manner at reasonably high levels of network. If contingency is not treated in this way, it runs rife and project overall times become so obviously long that the whole PERT system goes into disrepute. If the contingencies are clearly shown, the top management can leave or chop out as they decide. As the project proceeds there are bound to be changes in both the logic and progress of activities, different to that originally conceived.

This does not mean that anything is wrong, as the *Key*

Technique No. 7 states that planning must be a continuous process. In the seeking of the original information for activity times and resources, effort was employed to make sure that the information was good. Revision of the network is really the second test for the contributors. They must now honestly appraise their progress and state categorically, how far along the planned path they have actually proceeded. If the activity time was 20 weeks, 8 weeks have elapsed and re-examination of the activity reveals that further14 weeks of work are required, then it is vital that this information must come to light.

When one imagines that a PERT plan can contain from, say 100 activities up to many thousands, then the accumulation of "white lies", honest and wrong beliefs and any incompetence in revealing progress information can completely wreck the project, let alone the contribution PERT can make.

One of the problems about updating is that some of the initial enthusiasm in drawing up the logic for the first time, in sorting out some apparent management and company problems, however minor they may be, may have waned, and the updating seems to be a somewhat unnecessary labour. This is the moment when the Project Manager must prove his worth, by sticking to the correct course of action and regularly demanding, an efficient updating process from all contributors.

The physical work required, in displaying the results of updating may vary. Updating invariably implies new information availability, and if it is not done quickly, then the value of the exercise is lost. The above is not meant to imply that the smaller PERT system cannot also usefully be updated with the help of a computer.

14
Value for Money

Value may be defined as the relationship between function and cost. In all cases, value is greatest when the cost of obtaining a required function or service, at a particular time and place with essential qualities, is at a minimum provided :

- We have a product or process that functions.
- The product or process can be made available where and when the customer requires it.
- There is a demand for the product or process.
- The product or process functions to the customer's satisfaction and to the customer's specified degree of reliability.
- The product or process meets the customer's requirement with regard to eye-appeal, prestige of possession, and exchange value.
- The process or product meets all these requirements at the lowest possible cost, and is a profitable venture from the manufacture's viewpoint.

Before we take a look at the value question, we need to talk about the perceptions of cost conscious individuals.

(a) *Cost consciousness :* Lack of cost consciousness is an insidious happening, both for individuals as well as for businesspersons. In any organization, large or small, there is waste. Waste can occur in many ways, *viz.* : Slackness in demand, giving rise to excessive plant and materials; increased over staffing; slackness in supervision; overstocking of materials; slackness in budget control; poor product designs; inefficient production engineering and manufacturing; and low productivity.

Project Manager can help in optimizing value with the application of *Key Technique No. 5* and *Key Technique No. 6*, which are complementary to each other. Both these techniques are heightened in effectiveness by use of value engineering and value analysis. It is generally accepted that value engineering is the operation of optimizing value at the engineering development stage of the project, whereas value analysis is optimizing the value at manufacturing stage.

What is certain is that value engineering or value analysis will reduce costs, leaving the same or better quality and function, or it will improve quality and function while leaving the costs the same. It is by the market place than by the product cost, that product costs are dictated.

(b) *Value analysis :* Start up value analysis properly. It will reward you with figures of five to 15 per cent reduction in costs after expenses; sometimes much greater reduction without reducing the quality or reliability and probably improving on these.

What is the best way to start-up value analysis? There are several methods to achieving this. We can let the consultants come in to organize the job. Or, choose a man whom the company believes can start it up and let him get on with the job. Or, hire a man whom the company believes can do the job.

It is essential to possess the full faith that value analysis will succeed. Coordinate and enthuse others in the actual Value Analysis processes. This implies a thorough study by the value coordinator into value analysis techniques and their practical operation. The value coordinator must not be left entirely on his own. You must support his work, by seeing that the line management back his efforts.

(c) *Value analysis techniques :* Value analysis and cost reduction programmes are often confused. In practice, the two are different and one does not stop the other. Cost reduction is usually performing a given function at a lower cost by altering the materials or methods.

The central theme of Value Analysis is to question at all times the function of the equipment and every part within it. This involves a series of set questions, each of which is to be pursued in depth. These are as follows : Is the equipment necessary at all? Is the equipment function being performed at the lowest cost consistent with the quality and reliability? It is nothing to do with design by the committee.

When the equipment upon which value analysis is to be performed has been chosen, a team of appropriate experts is gathered together. A good working number is six to eight. A team smaller than six members loses impetus while larger number than eight gets ponderous. The procedure discipline consist six stages of work :

- Using the *Information Key Technique No. 5* to know the cost. Get all cost information on the product and product parts.
- *The Ideas Stage,* wherein brain storming will play an important role.
- *Ideas Assembly Stage,* when the ideas produced at the previous stage are investigated thoroughly and alternative solutions proposed.
- *The Recommendations Stage* where proposals are made by the value coordinator to the project team and any last changes included and the process is tidied up.
- *The Action or Implementation Stage,* when formal change requests are issued into the company's manufacturing system.
- *The Inspection or Monitor Stage*, when the value coordinator must check whether the changes are going forward properly and that eventually, the results are as expected.

(d) *Value engineering* : This term is usually applied to value analysis type work applied to the product before manufacture, that is in the complete design and development stages. There is no substitute for the utmost attack on the concept, application and design and development of a product. While the product is in very early stages the costs, methods of manufacture, performance and ultimate marketability are being fixed. This is the cheapest time to make changes; put the maximum design effort into the task and get it right.

Value Engineering requires a separate small group of people to investigate the design and help the designers in much the same way as we have explained under value analysis before. With Value Engineering the scope can be larger, as this is the time for the design and manufacturing processes to be turned inside out to find the best answers. There are ofcourse, always difficulties in time-scale as the time grinds inexorably on and a late product may be not be the required product or at least a poor seller. There is therefore, the greatest reason for maximum effort right from the beginning. All too often the effort is applied, when it is really too late.

The cooperation between the Value Engineering group and the design engineers must be very close and it is only to be expected, that the latter are entitled to see worthwhile results from the extra effort.

The domain of Value Engineers can be divided into the following areas:

- *The Basic Design function :* Nothing must be sacred in trying to tear apart the design to see if there is a simpler, cheaper, better way of doing the job. Brainstorming sessions, design reviews and committees all have their own place. The secret is to drive, drive, drive....in order to get the concept stage fully acceptable before moving on.
- The same applies to detailed specifications. *Attack the functions all the time.*
- *In the design and development stage*, apply all the technology knowledge at your disposal. Ready access is essential to information inside and outside the company. The right technology is one sure step to profits.

In detail, the areas of attack can range from overall function to say a plating process for a small part; to the Purchase Manager's well known graph of product cost, that is 20 per cent of the parts by quantity equals about 75 per cent of the cost. Refer to the Fig. 14.1 (given below). Then the value engineer must look at the high cost group of items, to get the maximum return over the least area.

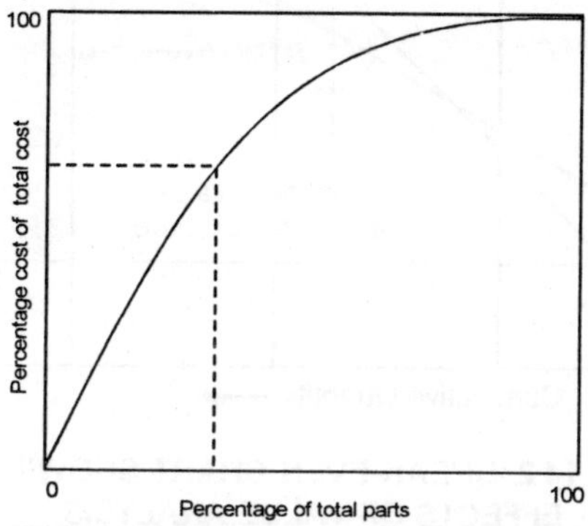

Fig. 14.1. PERCENTAGE OF TOTAL PARTS

Bought-out Parts or Items

The value engineer should always make sure that by correct specifications the company is getting the maximum benefit from bought-out items. Why were the parts bought-out in the first instance? Whether the answer is because the resources would be strained to do it or because of inability to carry out the technology required, the result is the same : Extra resources of men and machinery are being bought as required. If however the items are not specified correctly, there can either be an incredible waste of resources and/or the product function or cost is not planned. Encourage the subcontractor to join with you in achieving maximum value. Encourage him to use surefire ways and means of solving the problem and stimulate his interest in your problem by ensuring him fair profits with value control.

(e) *Value Control :* Value engineering is a vast subject in itself, the idea of value control is easy to appreciate. It is a state of never being satisfied unless costs are going down for a given

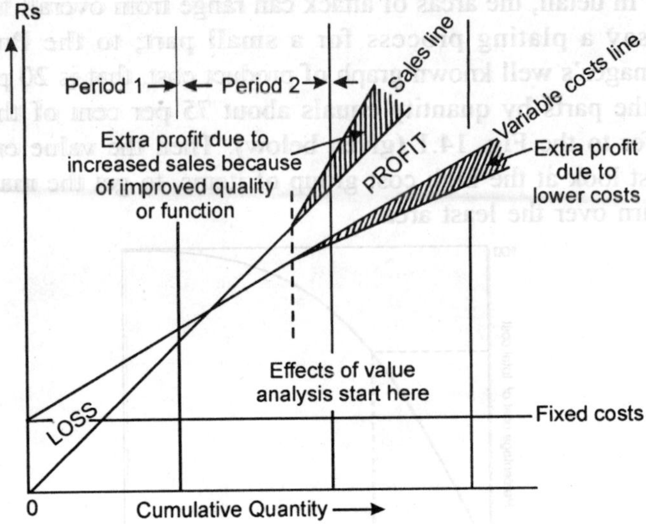

Fig. 14.2. BREAK-EVEN CHART SHOWING EFFECTS OF VALUE ANALYSIS

function and quality or function and/or quality are being improved for the same cost. Fig 14.2 (given above) shows the familiar "break even" chart with effects of quality and/or function adjusted.

15

The Contract

Is a contract necessary? A great many projects are carried out on behalf of a customer by a contractor. In such cases, a key document for the Project Manager is the contract. The first major point to consider is how far the contractor should be prepared to go without a contract. Some work will be done before the contract is to be prepared. This will involve preparing a tender and possibly even some engineering development or laboratory work to determine the feasibility of certain aspects of the plan. This however, must be done if there is to be any hope of securing the order. Once the decision to place an order is taken, how much work should be done before signing a contract?

If the project time-scale is tight and somehow it nearly always is, there is pressure to go ahead and start work without waiting for the paperwork. In some cases, this may be justified though it always contains an element of danger. However, if delay over the contract is due to a disagreement over terms or details of the contract, the disagreement will remain and may be strengthened as the work proceeds. If the situation compels the work to go ahead without a contract, try to obtain written heads of agreement on the basis of the relevant dates and agreement on the job to be accomplished, as well as the relevant dates and agreement on who pays for work done in anticipation of a contract.

The Contract Commitments

Although the formalities of drawing up the contract are unlikely to be the concern of the Project Manager, he is vitally concerned with some of its contents : Review of all dates quoted in the contract, Is it possible to meet them or has there been so much delay in evaluating tenders that all dates must be revised? Ideally, all dates quoted in tenders should be related to the date of Instruction to Proceed (ITP), for example completion on ITP date, plus 25 months.

Customers' Part in the Contract

It is worthwhile to consider if the project performance is any way dependant upon the customer. Customer dependencies should be extracted from your project PERT plan and listed with their dates. In a computer project, the customer may be required to have the building ready for the computer by certain date. It must be quite clear what state of readiness is required.

If the customer is required to provide a detailed specification of work to be done, it must be quite clear in the contractual documents what is to be supplied and when. It must be also clearly agreed what is to happen in the event :

- That the detailed specification differs materially from the invitation to tender.
- That on detailed scrutiny of the specification, the subcontractor finds serious flaws in it.

When a contract is undertaken on a cost plus basis, it is desirable to cover these points. When the customer is required to provide a detailed technical specification, enough care is to be exercised. If he is running late, he may try to pass off draft specifications in an unchecked manuscript state. When the final typed or printed specifications are received several weeks later; it may be found to differ significantly from the draft specifications. This can cause disruption in schedules.

If the contract is tied to fixed delivery date or a fixed price, it is absolutely essential to resist all pleas from the customer that the changes will be little ones and that the subcontractor should be reasonable. It is unreasonable to expect that there will be no changes to the specification during the life of the project. These however, must be kept to a minimum as changes can be very disruptive to progress.

Essential changes must be strictly controlled and recorded. The record must contain details of the changes, their effects and the date on which the customer and contractor agreed to the change. The implications on the cost and time-scale of the project must be evaluated and agreed. The effect of changes should be agreed by the customer in writing and should bear the signature of a member of the customer's staff who is able to authorize the expenditure.

Project Risks

The contractor should define in the contract the extent of the risk, he will bear. Where equipment is concerned, the precise point at which risk passes must be established. Similarly, risks pertaining to "on accidents on site" must be spelled precisely to fix its ownness. The Project Manager should try to identify all these risks. Agreement must be reached as to who carries the various risks at each stage in the project life. Once this is agreed, it should be a straightforward matter to arrange the necessary insurance.

Money Matters

Payment or part of the payment may be related to acceptance tests. In this case, there should be a contractual reference to the criteria and method of accepting testing. Progress payments enable the contractor to finance his work in progress. In the end the decision on whether there should be progress payments or not and how they should be phased is probably decided on the basis of which party has the easiest access to funds and which party can raise money at the lowest rate of interest.

In any project involving complicated machinery or complex systems, the customer must protect himself by clauses ensuring continuity of supply of parts or of maintenance where the contractor takes the responsibility of it. He should also ensure some agreement on price, preferably linking increases in price to some readily identifiable index. The contractor for his part is concerned to limit his future liability to maintain obsolescent machinery. Linked with the question of maintenance is that of documentation. The customer naturally, wants full and clear documentation. The extent of this should be agreed early on and adequate reference to it should be included in the contract. A linked point is the question of how many copies are required. There is also the question of training of customer's staff for operation and preventive maintenance of the equipment. These aspects tco should be included in the contract document.

Penalties

Penalties are a subject which is discussed quite a lot in connection with contracts. Penalties usually are referred to as payment of liquidated damages. The parties concerned consider what damage the customer will suffer in the event of late delivery and put a price on it. This means that should there be a delay in completion, all that need be established is the act of delay. The liquidated damages — or the penalty in common usage — becomes payable, provided the contractor does not allege the fault of the customer as the reason for the delay. In fact the presence of a "penalty clause", can act as a protection for a contractor.

Most contractors try to avoid a penalty clause in the hope that the customer will not take the recourse of the legal court to seek damages in the event of delay. If he does, they hope the responsibility for delay will be sufficiently unclear to protect them.

Where a subcontractor accepts a penalty clause there are some points he should watch. He should try to secure a period following the target delivery date, during which he will not be liable for penalties. He should try to exclude penalties for delay, as a result of circumstances beyond his control. Delays that are likely to result from the customer's failure to perform should be identified and excluded. The total size of penalty must always be restricted. Something between five and ten per cent of the contract price is quite common. The basis of say, 0.25 per cent for each week of delay to the maximum of five to ten per cent is normal.

When a customer insists on a penalty clause, the contractor should equally insist on placing on the customer any extra costs he may incur as a result of customer's default in performance. These extra or overrun costs as they are sometimes called can be considerable.

Linked to the question of penalty is that of cancellation. Normally, the contractor having signed a contract has no right to withdraw from the contract. The customer sometimes insists on the right to cancel in certain circumstances. Without provision for cancellation the project might drag on indefinitely without satisfaction to either party. If the project is within sight of satisfactory completion, it is unlikely that the customer will exercise his right to cancel, unless of course, he has had second thought about the value of the project.

16
The Financial Evaluation

One of the main preoccupations of management is the allocation of scarce resources. These resources include skilled management and staff, capital equipment and cash. Most projects are subjected to an evaluation before they are given the 'go ahead'. An essential part of this evaluation is the financial appraisal. Modern techniques go further than this. They go right inside a project and help management to decide on the precise shape of the project as well as highlighting those aspects of a project, which will warrant particular attention for management.

The more traditional ways of evaluating projects have been the Return On Investment Method and the Payback Period Method. Although these two traditional methods are still widely used, the advantage of the traditional methods is their simplicity, but they often provide a false basis for decision. Let us examine shortcomings of some the traditional methods of valuation.

(i) The Rate of Return (RR) or the Return on Investment Method

In this method, profit is expressed as a percentage rate of return on the initial capital investment. Expected profit is usually estimated often allowing for depreciation but before tax. A variation on this method is to take the average capital employed rather than the initial capital. To take a simple example, Rs. 10,000 is invested in a project with a 5 years life. The project earns Rs. 1,600 a year, before tax but after depreciation, in each of the 5 years, *i.e.* Rs. 8,000 in all. We assume that the residual value of the investment is nil at the end of the 5 years.

The rate of return is :

$$\frac{\text{Earnings}}{\text{Capital} \times \text{Number of years}} \times 100\%$$

$$= \frac{8{,}000}{10{,}000 \times 5} \times 100\% = 16 \text{ p.a. rate of return.}$$

The Rate of Return Method suffers from the following disadvantages : It takes no account of the timing of payments and receipts; and because the RR method takes no account of tax and is based on initial capital employed, it does not give a true rate of return on capital employed and is therefore, not a true yardstick by which to judge which project will be profitable.

(ii) The Pay Back Method (PB)

In this method, it is the number of years, which are taken to pay back the initial investment from the trading surplus. Normally the calculation is made ignoring both depreciation and tax. This method suffers from the following disadvantages : It takes no account of earnings which are expected to be received after the payback period; nor does it take into account the timing of receipts and payments within the payback period. Like the RR method, ignoring tax gives a false picture. A project with excellent payback period of 3 years, in gross terms may have a short life thereafter, and in after-tax terms may never be profitable.

Two projects A and B, both have an initial capital cost of Rs. 1,000 and both earn Rs. 1,200 over 6 years. The payback method indicates that both the projects have a payback period of 5 years. They will also have identical RR, that is Rs. 200 on initial investment of Rs. 1,000 or 20 per cent RR. As per the illustration given hereunder (Table 16.1), both PB and RR rate project A and B identically, although it should be clear that project B has a considerable advantage in timing of its earnings. After 3 years, it is expected to have earned Rs. 900, as against the Rs. 600 earned by project A.

To distinguish between projects we need a method, which will reflect the time value of money and for this purpose, the discounting methods have been developed.

TABLE 16.1

Years	Project A (In Rs.)	Project B (In Rs.)
0	1000	1000
1	200	350
2	200	350
3	200	200
4	200	50
5	200	50
6	200	20

(iii) Discounting Methods

The discounting techniques of investment appraisal overcome the disadvantages of traditional methods. This technique gives a value ranking to an investment project. Discounting techniques are founded on two simple concepts that of : Money has a time value. Money in the hand today, is worth more than the same money in the hand in a year's time. This reflects the fact that capital has a price that is interest and also that, the value of money is eroded by inflation. Investment in a project is concerned with cash, rather than with the entries in the conventional account books.

(iv) Net Present Value (NPV)

The NPV in a project is defined as "the value obtained by discounting separately for each year, the difference of all cash flows (outflow and inflow) accruing throughout the life of a project at a fixed and pre-determined interest rate". This difference is discounted to the point at which the implementation of the project is supposed to start. The NPVs obtained therefrom, for the years of the life of the project are added to obtain the project NPV. This can be depicted with the following equation :

NPV = (NCF – 1) + {(NCF – 2) + (a–2)} +{(NCF – 3) + (a –3)}+ …{(NCF –n)+ (a – n)}, where *(NCF – n)* is the net cash flow of a project in years *1, 2, 3, ..., n,* and *(a–n)* is the discount factor in years *2, 3, ..., n,* and appropriate to the discount rate applied.

Discount factors are obtained from present value tables. The discount rate (or cut-off rate) should be equal, either to the actual rate of interest on long-term loans in the capital market or to the interest rate paid by the borrower. Since capital markets frequently do not exist, the discount rate should reflect the opportunity cost of capital, that is : The possible return on the same amount of capital invested elsewhere. Or when expressed differently, the discount rate should be a minimum rate of return, below which an entrepreneur considers that it does not pay him to invest.

The discounting period should be equal to the life of the project, for example the useful life of the equipment is generally between 10 and 15 years, factory buildings will usually last for 30 to 40 years, while vehicles last for 4 to 5 years, etc. If the NPV is positive, the profitability of the investment is above the cut-off discount rate. If it is zero, the profitability is equal to the cut-off rate. A project with a positive or zero NPV can, thus be considered acceptable. If the NPV is negative, the profitabllity is below the cut-off rate, the project should be dropped.

To summarize, the NPV has great advantages as a discriminatory method when compared with the payback period or the annual rate of return, since it takes account of the entire life of the project and the timing of the cash flows. The NPV can also be considered as a calculated investment rate, which the profit rate of the project should at least reach. The shortcomings of the NPV are the difficulty in selecting the appropriate discount rate and that the NPV does not show the exact profitability rate of the project. For these reasons, it is advised to use the internal rate of return or IRR.

(v) Internal Rate of Return (IRR)

The internal rate of return (IRR) is the discount rate, at which the present value of cash inflows is equal to the present value of cash outflows. It is the rate at which the present value of the receipts from the project, is equal to the present value of the investment, and the net present value is zero. The procedure to calculate the IRR is the same as the one used to calculate the NPV. The calculation procedure begins with the preparation of a cash flow table. An estimated discount rate is then used to discount the net cash flow to the present value. If the NPV is positive, a higher discount rate is applied. If the NPV is negative at this higher rate, the IRR must be between these two rates.

If the discount rate still gives a positive NPV, the discount rate must be increased, until the NPV becomes negative. If the positive and negative NPV's are close to zero, a precise (the closer to zero, the more precise) and less time consuming way to arrive at the IRR, uses the following linear interpolation formula :

$I_r = I_i + PV (I_i - I_2)/PV + NV$, where I_r is the IRR, PV is the NPV (positive) at the low discount rate of I_i, and NV is the NPV(negative) at the high discount rate of I_2. The numerical values of both PV and NV in the above formula are positive. It should be noted that I_i and I_2 should not differ by more than one or two per cent.

The internal rate of return is obviously difficult to calculate and involves many trial and error exercises, but its greatest advantage is that it is a definite figure, based purely on a mathematical derivation from the values of outflows and inflows. It graphically portrays the essence of the investment strategy of the project without leaving any scope for the idiosyncrasies of the project formulation team.

Even in situations in which the comparison of alternative investment proposition is not involved, the interest rate of return (IRR) enables the Project Manager to have a good measure of generation of resources by the project. The proforma Operating Statement and the proforma Balance Sheet provide basic information, for the computation of the proforma Cash Flow Statement. The cash flow statement in its own turn yields the information, which is required for the computation of the internal rate of return (IRR).

The cash flow statement contains a number of entries, which reflect the flow of cash through a project. Not all these movements, however, constitute either outflows or inflows from the point of view of the internal rate of return. Identification of the flows, which are relevant to the calculation of the IRR, needs a lot of care and understanding. Form the suggested proforma of cash flow statement (Fig.16.2), it can be observed that cash was increased by an increase in share capital, increase in current liabilities, increase in long-term borrowings, increase in short-term borrowings, decrease in current assets, development rebates and subsidies and other items; in addition, cash flow increased by

TABLE 16.2

Cash Flow Statement

No.	Source of Cash	Item	Particulars	Year 1	Year 2	Year Nth
1.	Increase in share capital					
2.	Increase in current liabilities					
3.	Increase in long-term borrowings					
4.	Increase in short-term borrowings					
5.	Decrease in current assets					
6.	Decrease in current inventories					
7.	Operating profits before interest & tax					
8.	Depreciation charged to profit & loss a/c					
9.	Development rebate & subsides					
10.	Other items					
	Total A					
1.	Increase in fixed assets					
2.	Increase in inventories					
3.	Increase in current assets					
4.	Decrease in long-term borrowings					
5.	Decrease in short-term borrowings					
6.	Decrease in current liabilities					
7.	Inrterest payments					
8.	Taxation payments					
9.	Dividend payments					
10.	Other Items					
	Total B					
	Opening Cash Balance					
	Surplus/Deficit (A-B)					
	Closing Cash Balance					

operating profits before interest and tax, and by depreciation. Depreciation does not in fact constitute an outflow. As such, it has to be written back to obtain gross operating profits. Gross operating profits in effect constitute the inflows, which is relevant to the determination of the IRR of the project.

To identify the project outflows, it is necessary to consider the second part of cash flow statement relating to the application of cash. Cash is decreased by increase in current assets, decrease in long-term or short-term borrowings, and decrease in current liabilities and by payment of interest, tax, dividend, and other charges. It is also decreased by an increase in fixed assets and inventories. These last two items constitute the real outflows from the point of view of IRR.

The period of analysis depends on the economic life of the project. The operating statements, profit and loss account, balance sheet, and proforma cash flow statements are, however, prepared for the entire project execution stage, and for a limited number of years of the normalization phase, usually ten years. This period of ten years allows enough time for project to stabilize. The procedure provides a sufficiently accurate method of projecting outflows and inflows for the purposes of comparison of alternatives of computation of IRR.

Appendix

(A) Financial Appraisal seeks to assess the following

Reasonableness of estimate of capital cost; reasonableness of the estimate of working results; adequacy of the rate of return; and the appropriateness of the financial pattern.

(i) *Reasonableness of the Estimate of Capital Cost* — While assessing the capital cost estimates, efforts are made to ensure that : Padding or under-estimation of costs must be avoided; specification of machinery is proper; proper quotations are obtained from potential suppliers; contingencies are provided; and inflation factors are considered.

(ii) *Reasonableness of the Estimate of Working Results* — Is sought to be based on the following factors : A realistic market demand forecast; the price computations for inputs and outputs that are based on current quotations and inflationary factors; an appropriate time-schedule for capacity utilization; and the cost projections that distinguish between fixed and variable costs.

(iii) *Adequacy of Rate of Return*—The general norms for financial desirability are as follows: Internal rate of return at 15 per cent; return on investment at 20-25 per cent after tax; and debt service coverage ratio at 1.5:2. In applying these norms however, a certain degree of flexibility is shown on the basis of the nature of the project, the risks inherent in the project and the status of the promoter.

(iv) *Appropriateness of the Financing Pattern*—The institutions consider the following in assessing the financial pattern in a project, *viz.*: A general debt-equity ratio norm of 1.5:1; a requirement that promoters should contribute 12.50 to 22.50 per cent of the project cost; stock exchange listing requirements; and the means and the capacity of the promoter to contribute a reasonable share of the project finance.

(B) Economic Appraisal

The Economic Review looks at the project from the larger social point of view. The methodology adopted by the financial institutions for the purpose of economic evaluation (also referred to as Social Cost Benefit Analysis) is labelled as the "Partia Little Mirrless" approach. In addition to the calculation of the economic rate of return as per this approach, they also look to two other economic indicators, namely : (i) *Effective Rate of Protection*; and (ii) *Domestic Resource Cost*. Admittedly, the economic review done by the financial institutions is not very rigorous and sophisticated. Also the emphasis placed on this review is rather limited. However on the basis of the experience gained, the methodology would be improved and its emphasis increased.

(C) Managerial Appraisal

In order to judge the managerial capability of the promoters, the following questions are raised : How resourceful are the promoters? How sound is the understanding of the project by the promoters? How committed are the promoters?

(i) *Resourcefulness :* This is judged in terms of the prior experience of the promoters, the progress achieved in organizing various aspects of the project and the skill with which the project is presented.

(ii) *Understanding :* This is assesses in terms of the credibility of the project plan including *inter alia*, the organization structure, the estimated costs, the financing pattern, the assessment of various inputs and marketing programme and the details furnished to the financial institutions.

(iii) *Commitment :* This is gauged by resources (financial, managerial and other qualities) applied to the project and the zeal with which the objectives of the project, short-term as well as long-term are pursued. Managerial Review also involves an assessment of the caliber of the key technical and managerial personnel working on the project, the schedule for training them and the remuneration structure for rewarding and motivation.

(D) Key Financial Indicators

The key Financial Indicators used by the financial institutions while evaluating projects are the internal rate of return, the debt service ratio and the break-even point. In addition, some other indicators are employed as well. The manner in which, these indicators are calculated are discussed herewith :

(a) *Internal Rate of Return :* For calculating the Internal Rate of Return of a project, its cash outflows and cash inflows are defined as follows :

Cash Outflows

(i) *Outlay on fixed assets* will include the Cost of Project, that is the working capital margin and the interest during construction period.

(ii) *Outlay on current assets* will include current asset investment in the beginning, as well as additional investment in current assets on future.

Cash Inflows

(i) *Operating inflows* will include earnings before depreciation, interest and taxes (EBDIT).

(ii) *Terminal inflow* will include residual value of fixed assets, plus realizable value of current asset.

An illustrative stream of cash flows for a project would resemble one given in Table 16.3 below.

TABLE 16.3
Cash Flow for a Project

Year	Cash Outflows (In Rs. Lacs)		Cash Inflows (In Rs. lacs)		Net Cash Flow (In Rs. lacs)
0.	(a) Cost of project	(114.4	–		
	(b) Margin for working capital	(8.5	–		
	(c) Interest during construction	(5	–		
	Total	100.9	–		(100.9
1.	Investment in current assets	29.2	EBDIT	26	3.4
2.	Increase in current assets	5.8	EBDIT	32	26.3
3.	Increase in current assets	6.2	EBDIT	37	31
4.		—	EBDIT	37	36.6
5.		—	EBDIT	37	36.6
6.		—	EBDIT	35	35.3
7.		—	EBDIT	35	34.5
8.		—	EBDIT	34	33.8
9.		—	EBDIT	33	32.9
10.		—	EBDIT	32	—
	Residual value of land (4.7)				—
	Residual value of fixed assets (5.0)				—
	Residual value of current assets (41.2)				83

The internal rate of return for the above project is the value of (r) in the following equation :

$$100.9 + \frac{3.4}{(1+r)} = -\frac{26.3}{(1+r)^2} + \frac{31.0}{(1+r)^3} + \frac{36.6}{(1+r)^4}$$

$$+\frac{36.0}{(1+r)^5}+\frac{35.3}{(1+r)^6}+\frac{34.5}{(1+r)^7}$$

$$+\frac{33.8}{(1+r)^8}+\frac{32.9}{(1+r)^9}+\frac{83.0}{(1+r)^{10}}$$

The solving value of (r) is approximately 23 per cent. In general, if a project has an internal rate of return of 15 per cent or more it is considered worthwhile.

(b) *Debt Service Coverage Ratio*—The debt service coverage ratio is defined as :

$$\frac{\text{Profit After Tax+Depreciation+Other Non Cash Charges+Interest on Term Loans}}{\text{Interest on Term Loan+Repayment of Term Loan}}$$

Financial Institutions calculate the average debt service ratio coverage for the period during which the term loan is repayable as exhibited in Table 16.3 given above. Normally Financial institutions regard a debit service ratio coverage of 1.5 to 2 as satisfactory. If this ratio is less than 1.5 and the project is deemed otherwise desirable, a term loan of a longer maturity may be provided. By the same token, if this ratio is significantly higher than 2, the maturity period of the loan may be shortened.

(c) *Break Even Point* : The break even point for a project is calculated with reference to the year when the project is expected to reach its target level of capacity utilization, which is usually the third of the fourth operation year. To illustrate the calculation of the break even point consider the following data for the third year of a project, when it is expected to operate at 70 per cent of its installed capacity.

TABLE 16.4a

Debt Service Coverage Ratio

Rs. in million

	Year	1	2	3	4	5	6	7	8	9	10
A	Total Cash Actual										
1.	Profit after tax	0.27	0.81	1.35	1.13	0.99	0.99	0.99	1.01	1.02	1.04
2.	Depreciation	0.7	0.7	0.7	0.7	0.7	0.7	0.7	0.7	0.7	0.7
3.	Interest on term loan	1.18	1.18	1.07	0.93	0.78	0.64	0.48	0.33	0.19	0.04
	Total of A	2.15	2.69	3.12	2.76	2.47	2.33	2.17	2.04	1.91	1.78
B	Debt Service Requirement										
1.	Interest on term loan	1.18	1.18	1.07	0.93	0.78	0.63	0.48	0.33	0.19	0.04
2.	Repayment of term loan		0.4	0.8	0.8	0.8	0.8	0.8	0.8	0.8	0.4
	Total of B	1.18	1.58	1.87	1.73	1.58	1.43	1.28	1.13	0.99	0.44
	D.S.C.R. (A/B)	1.82	1.70	1.67	1.60	1.56	1.63	1.70	1.81	1.93	4.05
	Average D.S.C.R.	1.96									

A	**Variable Cost**	
	Raw materials & consumables	157.2
	Power	9.7
	Selling expenses	24.2
	Interest on working capital	5.8
		196.9
B	**Fixed Cost**	
	Wages & Salaries	12.0
	Factory overheads	0.6
	Administrative expenses	1.0
	Interest on term loans	10.7
	Depreciation	7.0
	Preliminary expenses written off	0.2
		31.5
C	**Sales Realisation**	241.9
D	**Contribution**	45.0

TABLE 16.4b
Debt Service Coverage Ratio

Using data in Table 16.4a, three measures of the break-even point (BEP) are calculated.

BEP in terms of production $= \dfrac{\text{Fixed cost}}{\text{Contribution}} \times \text{Target volume}$

$= \dfrac{31.5 \times 2016}{45} = 1411 \text{ tons}$

BEP in terms of installed capacity $= \dfrac{\text{Fixed cost}}{\text{Contribution}} \times \text{Target capacity utilisation}$

$= \dfrac{31.5 \times 70\%}{45} = 49\%$

BEP in terms of amount of sales $= \dfrac{\text{Fixed cost}}{\text{Contribution}} \times \text{Sales realisation}$

$= \dfrac{31.5 \times 241.9}{45} = \text{Rs. } 16.93 \text{ million}$

Other Indicators

Financial institutions look at the following indicators too :

Profit margin on sales $= \dfrac{\text{Net profit after tax}}{\text{Sales}}$

Return on owners equitity $= \dfrac{\text{Net profit after tax}}{\text{Promoters contribution + soft loan}}$

Fixed assets coverage ratio $= \dfrac{\text{Net fixed assets+capital work-in-progress}}{\text{Differed credits+Term loans+Debentures}}$
secured by first charge over fixed assets+ Other loans having pari passu charge over fixed assets

Debt equity ratio $= \dfrac{\text{Long term debt}}{\text{Equity}}$

Current ratio $= \dfrac{\text{Current assets}}{\text{Current liabilities}}$

RIO after taxes $= \dfrac{\text{Profit after tax+depriciation+Interest on term loan (1-tax rate)}}{\text{Cost of project}}$

RIO before tax $= \dfrac{\text{Profit before tax+Depreciation+Interest}}{\text{Cost of project}}$

17
Project Choice

Project choice is not merely a matter of listing Net Present Value (NPV) or Investment Rate of Return (IRR) rates, but a management judgment. Let us examine how management can successfully exercise its judgment in the selection of the project. Management must recognize the opportunities, a particular project has to offer.

The process of project selection may be considered logically under the following headings : The inventory of resources, the management framework, the detailed evaluation and recognizing the opportunities.

(i) The inventory of Resources

Broadly, the organization's resources are material–financial as well as human. Material resources cover property, stocks, tools and capital equipment. Where an organization is short of material resources, it can give adequate financial resources; buy what it needs in terms of material. However there are some material resources, which give particular strength to an organization. These include the material rights, which protect the existing know-how. There are some items of capital equipment's, which are expensive and have a long gestation period from initial order. The possession of such items may give a commanding position in a particular field.

Financial resources are of considerable importance. A strong financial position can be exploited to seize opportunities. The real strength lies in it's human resource – in it's people. A successful project-oriented organization depends upon variety of human skills – management and technical. Whatever are the strengths of an organization, it should be known to the management and this data bank should be continually updated.

(ii) The Management Framework

The management must formulate its aims and set them out sufficiently clearly. The management must try to set as objective a framework as far as is possible, for project selection. The target rate of return on investment is an important part of the management aim.

(iii) The Detailed Evaluation

If the project is in line with the organization's aim and it should go for detailed evaluation, which should be based on : Reliable and accurate information, use of sound techniques to evaluate the information and assumptions, evaluation of the resources required, the extent to which these will be available and continuous review.

The first stage of the evaluation is a project appreciation. The background to the proposed project is set down with a statement showing how it will benefit the organization. All the factors likely to affect the project are set down briefly. The main ways of tracking the project are described with their advantages and disadvantages. Finally, a recommendation is made for the continuing evaluation of the project and an outline of the method of execution to be adopted. The management can make its decision on whether to go forward with the project evaluation based on this initial project appreciation.

(iv) Reliable and Accurate Information

Project evaluation is known as an interactive process. In the early stages of project evaluation, only some of the information needed for planning is available. As the investigation of the project proceeds, every opportunity should be utilized to check that the initial facts are correct.

(v) The Assumptions

Almost more important than the basic facts are the assumptions made. No one can know with certainty, the trend of prices and sales over a period of several years ahead. Worst still, no one can predict with accuracy the future actions and attitude of the government, especially in tax matters and the differential encouragement to investment.

The most important assumptions are sales volume and pricing forecasts. This is specifically true of speculative projects like housing development projects, where the greater the degree of certainty about final marketing operation, the easier it will be both to finance the operation with additional loans and also, to decide on whether to go ahead with the project. Here the key assumptions are likely to be those relating to time. The probability of all these time assumptions must be carefully considered.

(vi) Sound Techniques

The techniques by which project planning information may be evaluated, have been referred to elsewhere in this book. The financial evaluation will have to be carried out using NPV and IRR techniques. The time and resource facts will have to be evaluated using PERT.

These techniques will be applied not just to the most probable facts and assumptions. A whole range of possibilities will be evaluated in order to highlight the risks and opportunities. However, we should take note of the danger of the evaluation, taking too long a time that the opportunity is missed. This happens, more so in the large bureaucratically controlled organizations.

(vii) Resources

An essential part of the evaluation is to calculate the phased requirements of the project. The possibility of obtaining additional resources from outside the organization must be considered. One of the prime concerns of management is the allocation of scarce resources. It is also a key factor in project selection.

(viii) Continuous Review

In project work, decision-making is a continuous process. It is wrong to think that a decision made once is the end of the task.

Assumptions and calculations must be continually reviewed and at planned intervals, the decision to go ahead and incur further expenditure must be consciously reviewed.

(ix) Recognizing the Opportunities

It is not worth going in for such projects, which do not show a satisfactory profit. There must be a careful analysis of what will be gained from taking on a project. It is also essential to find out at what cost — not only the direct costs — but also, the cost of profitable opportunities foregone.

The greatest opportunities arise from the recognition of new trends. Even though money is not the — be all and end all — of project selection, we must not forget that profits do matter. One of the most important factors leading to a profitable project is the careful and methodical search for the selection of the right project for the organization.

Successful project selection above all, depends on the correct evaluation of the organization's human resources and matching them, where these resources can be deployed to the maximum advantage.

18

More about PERT Technique

From the point of view of activity performance time estimation, project activity falls into two broad categories – probabilistic activities and deterministic activities. Probabilistic activities are of the nature of research and development work. The performance time of such activities cannot be anticipated with any degree of accuracy.

The Critical Path Method (CPM) as has been discussed earlier, primarily deals with situations where activity performance times are deterministic. A single time estimate is therefore used to define the activity performance time. Research and development projects have to fall back upon the PERT or a statistical method for determination of the mean activity performance time. The mean is obtained by using the formula :

$$t_e = \frac{a + 4m + b}{6}$$

where, a = Shortest estimated or optimistic performance time, which under similar conditions of work would be bettered, only in five out of 100 cases;

b = Pessimistic performance time or the longest estimated time which would be exceeded only by 5 out of 100 cases in similar conditions of work; and

m = The most likely time or the time, which will be taken more often than any other time.

The mean time estimate obtained from the formula is used in further scheduling calculations in the same manner as the deterministic activity time, that is t_e. Activity time estimates must

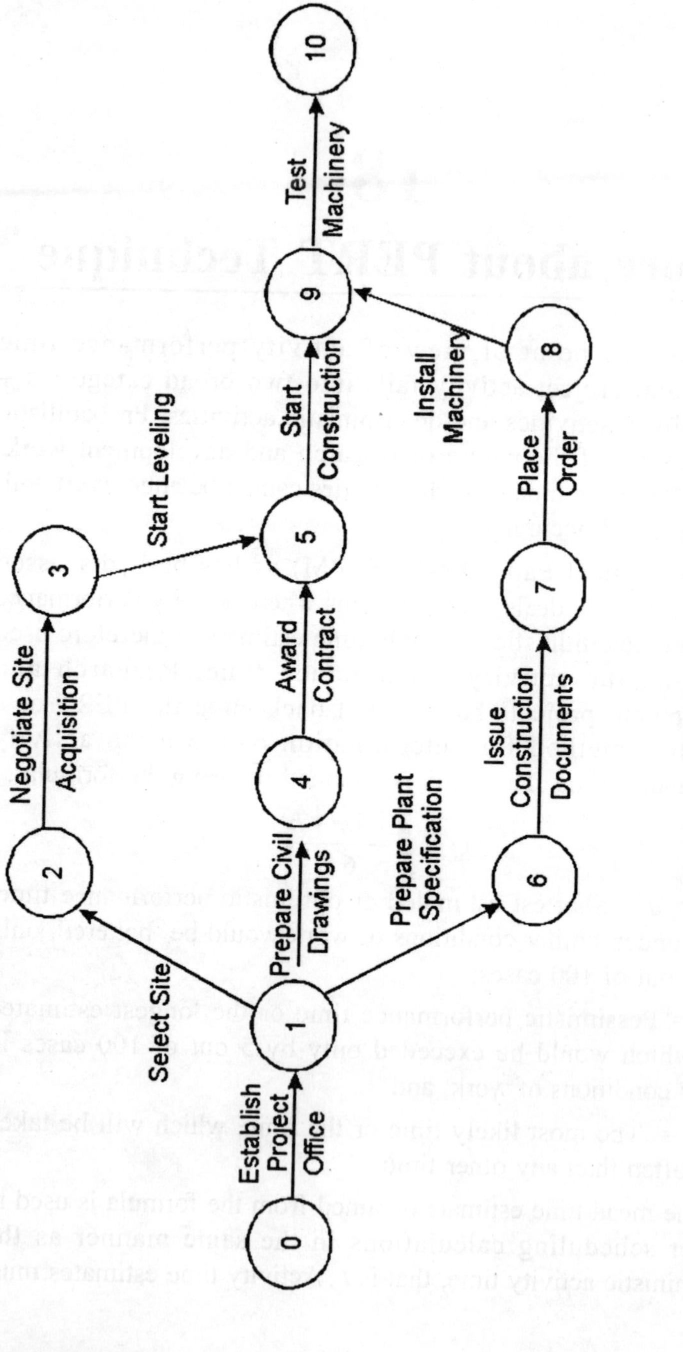

Fig. 18.1. PERT WITH ACTIVITY DESCRIPTION

be developed by project management team with help of those who have a first-hand knowledge of the concerned activity or who are working in a related field and have sufficient experience to make an authentic estimate. Time estimation is a difficult exercise, which involves the best judgment of an experienced hand.

Before proceeding to estimate the activity performance time of project activities, it is necessary to define the practice, which will be followed to identify the activities. Activities are sometimes identified by a descriptive narration inscribed along the activity arrow as in Fig.18.1. In other cases, activities are identified by capital alphabets written along the activity arrow. However, when activities runs into hundreds or more, activities are identified with the help of predecessor and successor events, for example, where i is the start of event and j, is an event end. This system of identification involves numbering of events in a careful and systematic manner. Event numbers must not be duplicated, nor should any two events be connected by more than one arrow.

TABLE 18.2

ACTIVITY PERFORMANCE TIME SCHEDULE

Activity Code	Activity Description	Activity Performance Time (wk)
0 to 1	Establish Project Office	6
1 to 2	Select Site	6
2 to 3	Negotiate Site Acquisition	5
2 to 4	Dummy	0
3 to 5	Site Leveling	4
1 to 4	Prepare Civil Drawings	4
4 to 5	Award Building Contract	4
5 to 9	Construct Building	12
1 to 6	Prepare Plant & Machinery specs	3
6 to 4	Dummy	0
6 to 7	Issue Contract Documents	4
7 to 8	Place Order for Plant Machinery	6
8 to 9	Install Machinery	8
9 to 10	Test & check Machinery	2

Two systems of numbering in current use are Random Numbering System and Sequential Numbering System. The sequential numbering system suffers from serious drawbacks as much as any incidental activity, which may be identified later and cannot be accommodated without disturbing the entire network. Hence the random numbering system is followed for the Project Formulation exercise.

With help of the event numberings and activity performance time-estimates, a complete project activity schedule can be drawn up as illustrated in Table18.2. Fig.18.3 is the network diagram, as it will look with event numberings at this stage.

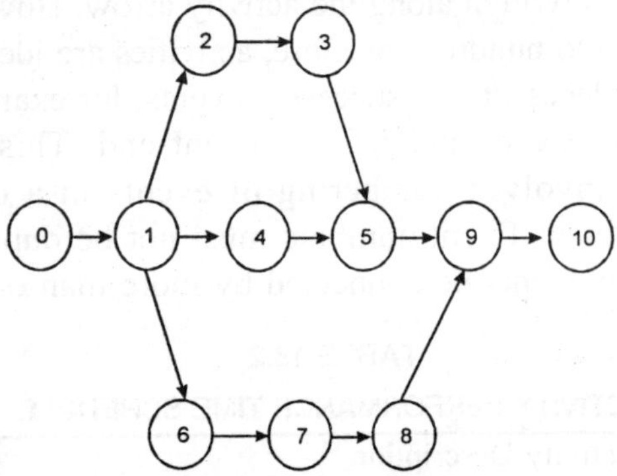

FIG. 18.3. PERT DIAGRAM WITH EVENT NOS. & ACTIVITY ARROWS

Forward Pass

It is the first operational exercise undertaken for scheduling computations with the help of network diagrams. The objective of this exercise is to determine the earliest start and finish of the constituent activities of a project. Activity performance times are generally specified in terms of elapsed time, that is in working days or weeks, in contradistinction to calendar days. After the forward pass, the computational results can be transferred to a calendar, in order to obtain a calendar-based schedule of operation.

Fig. 18.4 Illustrates forward pass indicating earliest expected activity finish time and occurrence time and Table 18.5 shows the "forward pass computation".

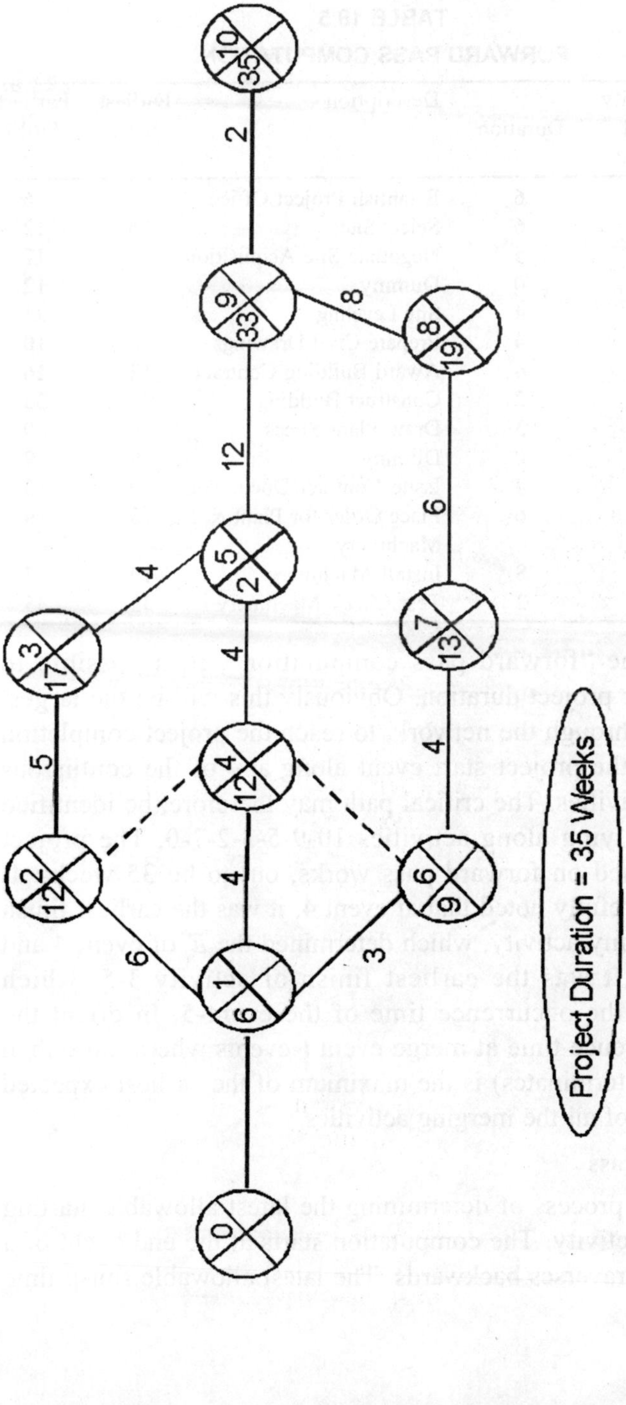

Fig. 18.4. FORWARD PASS — PERT CHART

TABLE 18.5

FORWARD PASS COMPUTATION

Activity Start Event	Activity End Event	Duration	Description	Earliest Start	Earliest Finish
0	1	6	Establish Project Office	0	6
1	2	6	Select Site	6	12
2	3	5	Negotiate Site Acquisition	12	17
2	4	0	Dummy	12	12
3	5	4	Site Leveling	17	21
1	4	4	Prepare Civil Drawings	6	10
4	5	4	Award Building Contract	12	16
5	9	12	Construct Building	21	33
1	6	3	Draw Plant Specs	6	9
6	4	0	Dummy	9	9
6	7	4	Issue Contract Documents	9	13
7	8	6	Place Order for Plant & Machinery	13	19
8	9	8	Install Machinery	19	27
9	10	2	Test Check Machinery	33	35

From the "forward pass computation", it is possible to calculate the project duration. Obviously this will be the largest time taken through the network, to reach the project completion event from the project start event along any of the continuous series of activities. The critical path may therefore, be identified as the path lying along activities 10-9-5-3-2-1-0. The project duration based on forward pass works, out to be 35 weeks. It has to be carefully noted that at event 4, it was the earliest finish time of dummy activity, which determined the E_t of event-4 and at event-5. It was the earliest finish of activity 3-5, which determined the occurrence time of the event-5. In effect the event occurrence time at merge event (events where more than one activity terminates) is the maximum of the earliest expected finish times of all the merging activities.

Backward Pass

It is the process of determining the latest allowable starting time of an activity. The computation starts at the end event of a project and traverses backwards. The latest allowable finish time of an activity is indicated in the right hand quadrant of the end event of the activity.

After the latest allowable finish time of the end event is determined, the latest starting time of an activity can be calculated by subtracting the activity duration time from the latest allowable finish time of the end event. If it so happens that no latest finish time of the end event is specified, then it is conventional to take latest finish time same as the earliest finish time of the end event. This is called the zero slack convention.

Table 18.6 illustrates the "backward pass computations" in tabular form while Fig. 18.7 (a) is the "network of the backward pass". Like in forward pass, the effect of the dummy activities on the backward pass calculations cannot be ignored. Dummies represent sequential interrelationship and as such have to be reckoned with while making scheduling computations.

Events 1, 2, 6 are *burst events*. At these points it is the least of the allowable start times of the succeeding activities, which determines the latest allowable completion time of the burst

TABLE 18.6

BACKWARD PASS COMPUTATIONS

Activity			Description	Latest Start	Latest Finish
Start Event	End Event	Duration			
0	1	6	Establish Project Office	6	0
1	2	6	Select Site	12	6
2	3	5	Negotiate Site Acquisition	17	12
2	4	0	Dummy	12	12
3	5	4	Site leveling	21	17
1	4	4	Prepare Civil Drawings	10	6
4	5	4	Award Building Contract	16	12
5	9	12	Construct Building	33	21
1	6	3	Draw Plant Specs	9	6
6	4	0	Dummy	9	9
6	7	4	Issue Contract Documents	13	9
7	8	6	Place Order for Plant & Machinery	19	13
8	9	8	Install Machinery	27	19
9	10	2	Test Check Machinery	35	33

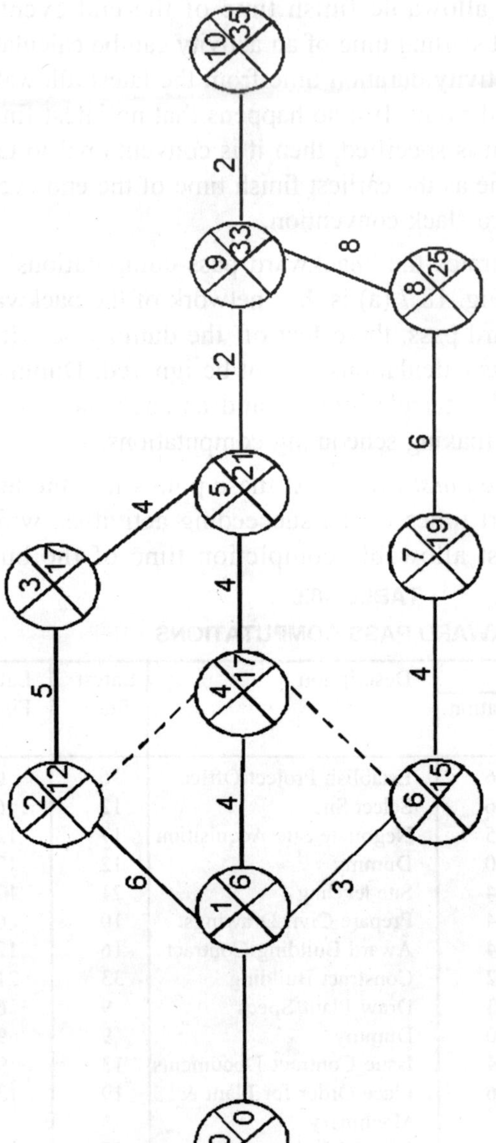

Fig. 18.7 (A) BACKWARD PASS LATEST ALLOWABLE START TIME & LATEST ALLOWABLE EVENT OCCURANCE TIME

event. The latest allowable completion time helps in determining the extent to which an activity may be delayed, without causing any upset in the completion time of the project.

Determination of "Slack"

The total activity slack and the activity free slack are two types of slacks, that are most commonly encountered in scheduling computations.

(a) *Total activity slack :* It is the time interval between the earliest expected start and the latest allowable start of an activity, for example referring to Table 18.7 (b), event-4 to event-5 = 17-12=5. In the same manner, it can also be computed from the values of the latest allowable finish and the earliest expected finish times of activity. Referring again to information in Table 18.7 (b), it is 21-16 = 5.

(b) *Activity free slack :* It occurs at merge points. It is the time interval between the earliest finish of an activity and the earliest start of the succeeding activity, for example the Free Slack (FS) at event 1-4 = 12-10 = 2. The activity free slack

TABLE 18.7 (B)
FORWARD & BACKWARD PASS COMPUTATIONS

Activity Start Event	Activity End Event	Duration	Description	ES	LS	EF	LF	Slack
0	1	6	Establish Project Office	0	0	6	6	0
1	2	6	Select Site	6	6	12	12	0
2	3	5	Negotiate Site Acquisition	12	12	17	17	0
2	4	0	Dummy	12	17	12	17	5
3	5	4	Site Leveling	17	17	21	21	0
1	4	4	Prepre Civil Drawings	6	13	10	17	7
4	5	4	Award Building Contract	12	11	16	21	5
5	9	12	Construct Building	21	21	33	33	0
1	6	3	Draw Plant Specs	6	12	9	15	6
6	4	0	Dummy	9	17	9	17	8
6	7	4	Issue Contract Documents	9	15	13	19	6
7	8	6	Place Order for Plant & Machinery	13	19	19	25	6
8	9	8	Install Machinery	19	25	27	33	6
9	10	2	Test Check Machinery	33	33	35	35	0

KEY

ES : Earliest Start; EF : Earliest Finish; LS : Latest Start; LF : Latest Finish.

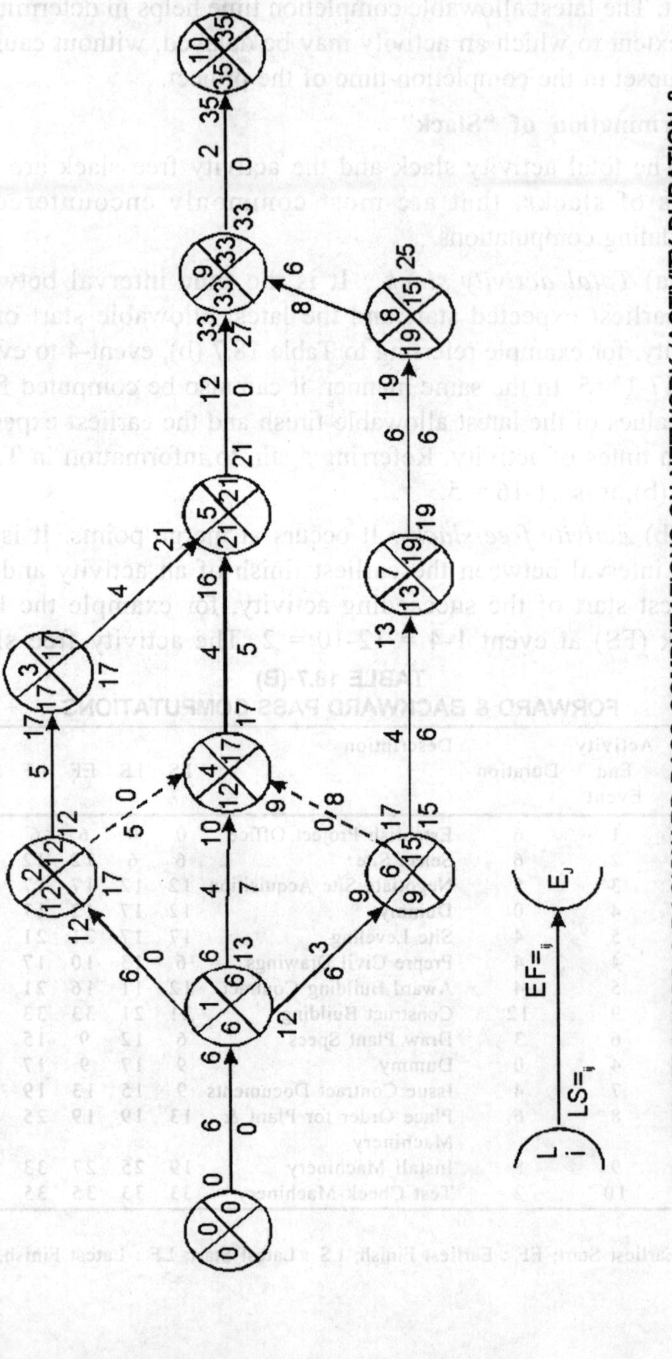

Fig. 18.8. FORWARD & BACKWARD PASS COMPUTATIONS ON NETWORK (ACTIVITY DURATION & TOTAL FLOAT ARE ALSO INDICATED)

indicates the time by which the completion time of an activity can be delayed, without affecting the occurrence of any succeeding event or activity.

The Critical Path

It can be identified in terms of total slack by identifying the path having the least slack. In case zero slack convention is used, the critical path will be the path having zero slack. The Table 18.7 (b) contains a full analysis of the scheduling computation of the network examined in Fig.18.8.

Time-Cost Trade-off

During the course of project formulation, it is sometimes observed that the project duration time calculated based on normal activity performance time-estimates, do not conform to "time constraints" of the project. Time-constraints generally arise because the project has of necessity to meet a particular deadline. It may also happen that a series of activities of project gets delayed beyond a critical level and consequently, a time-constraint develops for the entire project. In case of projects involving heavy indirect charges, a question may arise regarding the feasibility of reducing the project duration, so as to minimize the sum total of the direct and indirect charges. CPM time-cost trade-off procedure provides a ready technique for meeting such situations.

Project activities which are the basic constituents, of the work plan of a project have a normal activity time. This is the time which an activity can take under normal conditions, that is in situations involving the minimum expenditure of resources and consequently minimum cost. The project duration estimates developed with the help of forward pass, determine the normal time which a project will take, that is the time which the project will take at minimum activity cost. Besides the direct activity cost, a project also incurs indirect costs. Indirect costs consist of standing and supervision charges and interest charges on cumulative investments. In the case of capital-intensive projects, the incidence of the indirect charges is heavy. The project total cost consisting of the sum of direct and indirect costs, therefore, may not be minimal if the project duration time is determined on the basis of normal activity costs alone. It may be possible to buy time, particularly along the critical path in the project in such a manner as to reduce the total project cost.

In order to reduce the length of the critical path, time has to be bought on one or the other of the constituent activities of the critical path. By providing additional and more expensive resources, it is possible to reduce the activity performance time of a particular activity. There are certain constraints to make it impossible to reduce the activity below a particular minimum. The minimum activity time is known as the **crash performance time.**

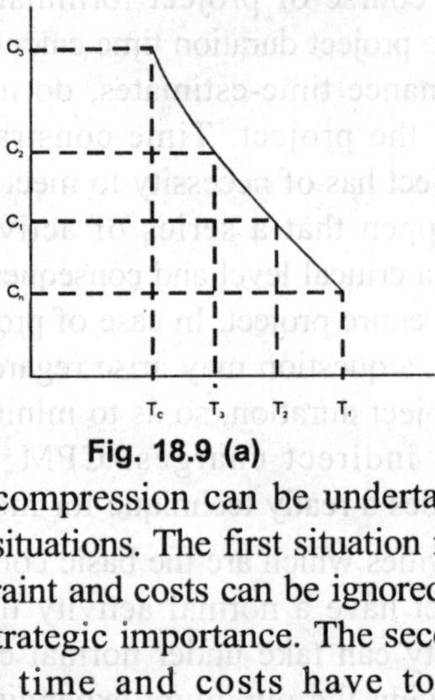

Fig. 18.9 (a)

Project duration compression can be undertaken under two distinctly identifiable situations. The first situation is the one when time is the only constraint and costs can be ignored. This situation arises in projects of strategic importance. The second situation is the one when both time and costs have to be reckoned with. When time is the only constraint, the process starts with development of time-cost estimate to establish cost of buying time. Simultaneously, crash activity time for critical path activity should be estimated. If the normal cost of an activity is C_n, the normal duration is T_n and the crash activity cost is C_c, then :

$$\Delta t = T_n - T_c$$

$$\Delta c = C_c - C_n$$

$$\frac{\Delta t}{\Delta c} = \frac{\text{cost}}{\text{unit time}}$$

In cases where there is only one critical path, activity with the lowest time slope *C/T* is not selected for augmentation, until the crash activity time for the activity is reached. The forward pass exercise helps in the determination of the new project duration time. If the new duration is less or equal to the desired duration, the exercise is stopped.

When two or more paths are critical, it becomes necessary first to identify the common activities and after grouping them, determine the optimal augmentation along this group and its cost-time slope. The results can be represented graphically, thus :

In the second solution, when time and costs are both critical, it is obviously to determine the value of duration time which will make the sum total of direct and indirect costs minimum. The graphical relationship between time and costs are similar to earlier situations. The project indirect costs are superimposed on the earlier graph. This graph is in the nature of a straight line. The points where the two graphs interact generally gives the lowest total cost point for the project. This situation is illustrated in Fig.18.9 (b) below. It is obvious from this illustration, that the project total costs will be lowest if the project duration is T.

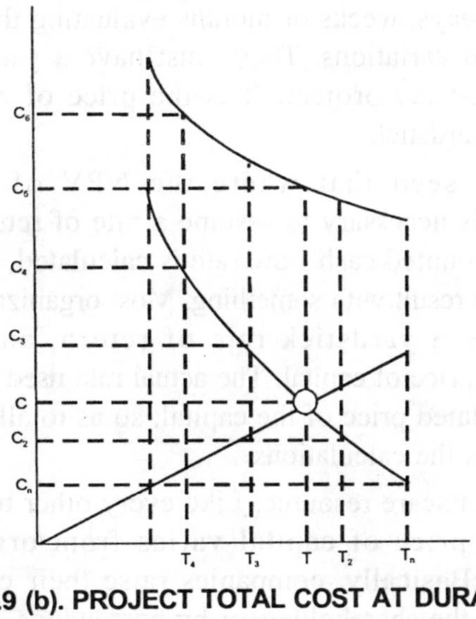

Fig. 18.9 (b). PROJECT TOTAL COST AT DURATION

19

The Price of Capital

No business can afford to pay more for its capital, than it can earn on it. Even though nobody would dispute this statement, still every year, great many companies go out of business because they earn less on their capital than they have to pay interest for it. A frequent cause for this is that the true price of capital has not been assessed.

Projects involve capital expenditure. Well-planned projects are carefully evaluated to ensure that they are worthwhile. Much time and effort is expended in arriving at the Net Present Value (NPV) or Discounted Cash Flow (DCF) rate for the project. For very large projects, highly qualified staff with computers is employed for days, weeks or months evaluating the project with all its possible variations. They must have a yardstick against which to judge the project. It is the price of capital, which provides this yardstick.

We have seen that where the NPV of a project is calculated, it is necessary to assume a rate of return on capital. When the discounted cash flow rate is calculated, it is necessary to compare the result with something. Most organizations handling projects have a yardstick rate of return, and this is the organization's price of capital. The actual rate used may be higher than the calculated price of the capital, so as to allow for certain uncertainties in the calculations.

Capital is a scare resource. Like every other resource, it has a price. The price of capital varies from organization to organization. Basically, companies raise their capital by two means – from the shareholders or by borrowings.

I. Shareholders' Capital

The shareholders of a company fall broadly into two classes – preference and ordinary. Preference shares are issued at a fixed rate of interest and do not participate in the profits of the company beyond their fixed rate of interest. Ordinary shareholders are the owners of the company. They contribute additional capital in one of the two ways. A company can make a new issue of ordinary shares, slightly below the market value of the existing shares and offer them as "rights" to existing shareholders. True cost of ordinary shares to a company, is considerably more than the immediate dividend yield. If the company does not pay out full profits in a year in the form of dividend, then the balance is added to the capital of the company. This balance is known as the "retained earnings". It is a cheap way of obtaining fresh capital. The return to ordinary shareholders is made up in the form of both the dividend and the capital gains. Capital gains result from putting the retained earnings to work for the company, which in turn generates increased earnings for the company. The increased earnings in turn, result in increase in the share price.

II. Borrowed Capital

Borrowed capital may take many forms. The most common are bank overdrafts and loans, issue of debentures and loan stocks, as well as mortgages on properties. The amount that can be borrowed depends upon the credit status of the borrower, the nature of business, etc. What is the price of capital for a particular project? The normal practice is to calculate the average cost of the new capital to the company and use this, as a yardstick against which to judge all projects.

It is sensible to calculate a price of capital for the particular project rather than take a company average. This is also true for projects with heavy loan financing, where a DCF calculation should be done on an equity basis. In this type of discounted cash flow calculation the loans, their interest and repayment are treated as cash flows and the DCF return is calculated on the equity capital. This discounted cash flow return is, then compared against the company's price of equity capital.

Conclusion

The price of capital is an essential yardstick, against which to measure the profitability of projects. In small concerns, it is a figure in the minds of the management. In large organizations, it is a figure, which should be publicized to the Project Managers. The price of capital is not just an esoteric figure to be considered by company management and calculated by their accountants. It is a tool of Project Management. Project Managers must be concerned not only with the execution of their projects, but also with their profitability.

In order to tell whether a project is profitable, one requires a yardstick against which to measure it. *That yardstick is : The Price of Capital*.

20

Successful Project Management: The Golden Rules

In this book, we have suggested various techniques that will be useful to Project Managers. In this chapter, we present some golden rules to guide them along the path of successful Project Management.

Golden Rule 1 : Know Your Objectives

Why is the project being undertaken? The Project Manager will make many decisions in the course of the project. The decisions are more likely to be correct, if he has a clear idea of his objectives. This is a problem not only for him, but also for the company's management to whom he reports. Confusion about objectives can lead to some odd results. Any incentive of rewards bestowed on the Project Manager for the completion of the project within the stipulated time schedule, should be in consistence with the project objectives. Else, it may lead to the Project Manager sacrificing performance standards or overspending his budget.

Golden Rule 2 : Define The Project Requirements

Once the objectives of a project are clear, it is essential to go on to define the project requirements in detail. This is, of critical importance. If you cannot define what you are going to do, you are unlikely to do it. The form of definition may vary, depending on the industry and on the practice within the industry. Each party to the project must be fully aware of his part in the project definition.

Experienced Project Managers are aware of the need for clear and unambiguous definition of requirements. They are more often, subject to strong pressures to be "reasonable". It goes without saying that each party involved in a project, should understand the same thing from the project definition. Lack of common understandings of the project definition, is often a source of project problems and recrimination. The project definition should be committed to paper and must be controlled by documents. Not every little detail need be specified, but the requirements must be specified down to a level of detail that permits firm estimates of cost, time-scale and performance to be made. A fully documented and agreed project definition is the basis for a successful project.

Golden Rule 3 : Keep Firm Control Over Changes in Requirements

In a project of any size, there will be some change in the requirements during the course of the project. Change may be necessary as a consequence of the end-user requirements. The laws may change and make more stringent demands on the field of safety or environmental pollution. There may also be circumstances, where the main contractors may want to make a change, in order to take advantage of some trade-off of cost or time against performance. Every change can potentially affect the cost or performance or completion date of the project.

It is essential to have a strict and formal procedure for considering all proposed changes. Each one should be evaluated in terms of its potential impact on cost, time-scales and performance. These must be formally considered by the Project Manager. Subject to his authority, he may either reject the proposed change(s) or authorize a formal amendment to the baseline definition of requirements. Where he does not have the authority to do so, he will have to refer the change with a statement of impact and his recommendation to the appropriate authority. The emphasis on change control is essential, especially for large and complex projects. In considering the impact of change, we must also consider its effect on the ease of use, as well as maintenance.

Golden Rule 4 : Plan Soundly

At the foremost, it is essential to soundly conceive the plan. Before any work starts, there should be a macro level plan, which takes the project right through to its final stage. If time-scales are tight, it may be necessary to order some materials almost at once. As you plan a project, you must try to foresee everything that could go wrong and prepare contingency plans.

More generally, it pays to look hard at all your external dependencies. Some activities are dependant on events outside our control, such as the completion of work by contractors or deliveries from suppliers or goods and services which may have to come from other divisions in the company. For projects that are particularly time-critical, we may have to spend lots of money on contingency plans. In such situations, the Project Manager has to make a series of difficult decisions, as he trades-off the costs of contingency arrangements against the likelihood costs of project delay.

Golden Rule 5 : Define Responsibilities Clearly

In actual practice, the pride, status, ambition, personal and organizational problems may arise, leading to blurring of responsibilities. Changes both in the project organization itself and in the environment in which project is implemented can cause confusion. For most projects, the senior management can carry out their obligation to avoid confusion of responsibilities, by appointing a Project Manager and setting him objectives about what is to be achieved, at what standards, at what cost and by when. The Project Manager in turn, must ensure that every one concerned in the project knows the extent of his responsibilities.

Golden Rule 6 : Ensure A Good Flow of Information

Timely and accurate information, is essential for the success of every project. The Project Manager needs to set-up his own project reporting system, in order to see that he gets the information he needs and when he needs it. As he does not have the time to deal with all the information generated by the project, he must be selective. A good start will be concentrating on the activities that are on the critical path of the project and ensuring an adequate flow of information about these.

Wherever there is an external dependency he should makes sure, that he has adequate information about its progress. The Project Manager should not wait for information. Instead he should go and get it, after seeing the progress for himself. For key items, it is vital to supplement written reports by factory or site visits. The Project Manager should be objective in receiving information. He must ensure that that senior management is always kept informed, on important changes that may effect the completion date, the cost as well as the performance.

Golden Rule 7 : Identify and Concentrate on Critical Items

There is a well-established management law that pronounces –80:20 rule. The rule elucidates that in any situation, 80 per cent of the problems come from 20 per cent of the activities. The rule also professes many variations and applications; like spend 80 per cent or more of your time on 20 per cent of critical items and the balance on routine items. Your network helps you to select the critical activities. However, any activity that slips through significant amounts of float must be investigated before it reaches the critical stage.

Golden Rule 8 : Select Subcontractors with Care

The most important aspect of a tender from a subcontractor is not the quoted price, even though generally, tenders are decided on the basis of "price". The most important aspects of this golden rule is seeking answers to the following questions : Can the subcontractors be relied upon to stay in business? Will he do what he has been asked to do, in terms of performance and delivery? Can he be relied upon to help you at a cost, if the project runs into difficulties?

Golden Rule 9 : Recognize the Need for Trade-Offs

Projects seldom run according to the schedule. That is why the Project Manager is required. One of his key functions is to examine problems and see to what extent they can be overcome by trading-off cost against time and performance. Normally any delay can be overcome, if it is seen early enough, either by additional expenditure or by a reduction in performance. Similarly, cost can be reduced by permitting delay and or reducing specification, although a delay in itself begets some additional costs. Performance can sometimes be improved, by procuring more time and spending more money. The Project Manager must recognize, that no plan can be cost fool-proof. He must be prepared to make trade-offs between various activities within his project, as well as overall trade-offs between cost, time and performance.

Golden Rule 10 : Avoid Unnecessary Risks

Plan sensibly and right through. Avoid planning unproven equipment, wherever possible. In a large, state-of-the-art projects, where you are doing new things, try to be evolutionary rather than revolutionary. Only embrace new, unusual or special facilities, where it is impossible to use what has been already used and proved.

It is possible to manage projects successfully, by using key techniques and following golden rules. *The result is a Successful Project Management*.

Bibliography

Baumgartner J.S., *Project Management*, Irwin, U.S.A.,1964.

Cleland D.J., *Why Project Management*?, Business Horizons, Winter, 1964.

Elliot J.W., *Economic & Analysis for Management Decisions*, Illinois, 1973.

Hackney J.M., *Control and Management of Capital Projects*, Wiley, 1965.

Helfert R.A., *Techniques of Financial Analysis*, Illinois, U.S.A, 1972.

Huitson A. and Keen J., *Essentials of Quality Control*, Heinemann, 1965.

Lowe C.W., *Critical Path Analysis by Bar Chart, Business Books*, 1969.

Moder J.J. and Phillips C.R., *Project Management With CPM and PERT*, New York, Chapman & Hall, 1964.

Simons L., *The Basic Arts of Financial Management*, London, 1974.

Taylor W.J. and Walting T.F., *The Basic Arts of Management*, 1972.

Taylor W.J. and Walting T.F., *Successful Project Management*, Business Books, 1979.

Wearne S.H., *Control of Engineering Projects*, Arnold, 1974.

Whithouse G.E., *Project Management Techniques, Industrial Engineering*, 1973.